Case studies in classroom management

Case studies in classroom management

David M. Galloway

Longman London and New York

Longman Group Limited
London
Associated companies, branches and representatives
throughout the world
Distributed in the United States by Longman Inc., New York

© Longman Group Limited 1976

First published 1976

Set in Monotype Plantin by Western Printing Services
Limited, Bristol, England and printed in Great Britain
at The Spottiswoode Ballantyne Press, by William Clowes
& Sons Limited, London, Colchester and Beccles

Library of Congress Cataloging in Publication Data

Galloway, David M
  Case studies in classroom management.

  Bibliography: p.
  Includes index.
  1. Classroom management—Case studies.
I. Title.

LB3013.G32   371.1'02   76-10348
ISBN 0-582-48562-2

Contents

Acknowledgement
The histories of Billy and George are based on part of an article by the author: "A Behavioural Approach to Treatment", published in *Therapeutic Education*, 1975, No. 2.

Introduction

These case histories are about the daily challenge of classroom teaching. They show how problems can develop in fundamentally normal children, and in many cases they illustrate how imaginative teachers have found ways to help children with intransigent learning and behaviour problems without labelling them ESN or maladjusted, and without removing them to a special school. Each history shows that there is no simple explanation; when a child puzzles or exasperates his teachers, whether because of learning or behavioural difficulties, we need to look at the total situation. The home, the teacher, the other children and the child himself may each have contributed to the problem, and any or all of them may need to be involved in the solution.

At a time of increasing concern about academic standards and growing demands from teachers' associations as well as the popular press for problem children to be segregated into special schools, it is salutary to hear how ordinary class teachers often succeed in providing *special* education of the highest quality. Diagnosis and treatment are not the prerogative of the so-called expert. The class teacher has an essential role in assessing a child's needs; in cooperation with the educational support and advisory services – Education Welfare Officer, psychologist, school doctor, etc. – he/she can make systematic and practical plans to help the academic or social misfit.

Each case history is preceded by two or three "main points", intended to focus the reader's attention on the crucial issues. At the end of each history, questions are provided which can form the basis for discussion. The questions deliberately cover a wide range; some are suitable for students in their first year or two of training; others could be used in sensitivity training for teachers specialising in counselling or pastoral care. Cooperation between schools and other agencies is a recurring theme.

Matthew

Main Points

1 If a child is too anxious about a subject he may be unable to make any progress in it. A vicious circle is established in which failure leads to anxiety, and this in turn makes further failure more likely.

2 Even in a good home with caring parents the interactions between different members of the family can contribute towards a child's learning difficulties.

3 A child's own temperament and personality have a major influence on how successfully he copes with potentially stressful situations.

"I'm not so bothered about Matthew's reading," said Mrs Fraser, Matthew's class teacher, "it's his anxious look and nervousness that worries me." "He's been like it ever since he came up from the infants two and a half years ago," said the head teacher, who happened to overhear. "We see his mother every term on open night, and she strikes me as the worrying sort."

Mrs Fraser supposed that Matthew might have inherited some of his anxiousness from his mother, but this seemed a rather feeble explanation, and it did not give her any clue about how to help him. He was certainly a puzzling child; at times he would concentrate hard and produce work of a high standard, but at other times a worried look would come over his face, he would visibly withdraw into himself, start biting his nails, refuse to make eye contact, and generally look like a nervous wreck. The lesson in which this was most evident was English; Mrs Fraser had him in a remedial group for this, and although there were only six other children he was seldom willing to attempt anything. The previous week she had spent half an hour teaching him about the final "e", but only yesterday when the word "fine" had occurred in his reading book a look of glazed apprehension crossed his face and he was totally unable to read it. He enjoyed drawing, though he always resisted attempts to persuade him to start painting, and preferred to confine himself to a lead pencil. He showed some interest in craft work and joined the school's free drama group. He was competent at PE, but showed little enthusiasm. He had no sisters, but one brother who was a year and a half younger than he. Paul was a noisy, exuberant little boy, who quickly made his presence felt wherever he went. Most of his teachers thought of him as a likeable pest, though his previous form teacher thought he was just a plain pest! The two boys seemed quite unalike in temperament and behaviour, but at least on the surface they seemed fond of one another. Matthew, quite unnecessarily, adopted a somewhat protective attitude towards Paul, and often spoke affectionately about him when talking to Mrs Fraser. However, once when she was doing playground duty she had noticed Matthew watching Paul with a look of intense jealousy and resentment on his face. He had happened to look up and see her, and was immediately covered in confusion, which he tried unsuccessfully to hide by joining in the game Paul was playing. The following week he was at pains to tell her about the nice things that Paul and he had done together during the weekend.

The next open night Mrs Fraser made a point of having a longer talk than usual with Matthew's mother. She learnt quickly that Mrs Gilly also was worried about Matthew. "He was terribly slow learning to talk," she said, "he could only say a few words when he started school, even though he understood everything that was said to him. The infant school told me to take him to speech therapy, and he had treatment for about a year. He was a lot better then, though he still couldn't explain himself very well, but they said he had learnt enough to carry on making progress without extra help." Mrs Gilly said she had stopped worrying when Matthew started to talk better, but when he left the infants, and she realised that he still couldn't read at all she had started to worry again, and had been trying to teach him every evening at home. She had to admit though that both Matthew and she hated these sessions, and they seemed to be making a big gulf between them. "Sometimes a haunted look comes into his eyes, and he starts crying, and I feel like crying myself, but he's got to learn to read hasn't he ?" Mrs Fraser asked how Matthew and Paul got on together at home. "It's difficult to tell," replied Mrs Gilly. "They seem to get on all right, but I sometimes wonder whether Matthew wouldn't really like to put Paul in the dustbin. It's so difficult, because really Paul's much better at most things than what Matthew is, and Matthew knows it, especially when it comes to reading, and Paul often tells him the words."

The next day Mrs Fraser rang up the speech therapy clinic, and was told that although Matthew's verbal comprehension was up to his age when he started school his expressive language (his ability to express himself in words) was considerably retarded. This could undoubtedly have hindered his progress in his first year or two at school. "We didn't ask the psychologist to see him," said the speech therapist, "because apart from his language difficulty it seemed fairly clear that he was of normal intelligence and we didn't think his emotional problems were greater than those of our other children." Mrs Fraser agreed with this estimate, and felt that she was at last starting to understand Matthew better. Because of his language problems he had been unable to make much progress for his first year or two; by the time speech therapy had helped him over this he was already accutely conscious that he was behind the other children in his class at reading.

At precisely this stage, noisy, exuberant little Paul had started school, and as the infant school had been vertically grouped was put in the same class as Matthew where he promptly proceeded to dominate his older brother; Mrs Gilly had told Mrs Fraser that when Paul started school he had taken great delight and pride in the fact that he could read some of the Ladybird books, whereas Matthew could not. The effect of this on Matthew was to make him opt out of competition with Paul, with the result that the gap between them widened. In the junior school the classes were organised by age, but by this time Matthew felt convinced that he could not learn to read. All the teachers who knew him agreed that he was a conscientious child, probably too conscientious, thought Mrs Fraser. Whereas another child in her class seemed to protect himself from the fear of failure by adopting a brazen couldn't care less attitude, Matthew seemed almost paralysed with anxiety. "He's his own worst enemy, really," remarked the head teacher.

Mrs Fraser felt that his mother's well-intentioned efforts to help him were probably having the opposite effect; she decided that Matthew needed to make a completely fresh start with reading, and introduced Stott's Reading Apparatus into her group. When Matthew discovered that he was no longer expected to read books – the things he had been failing with for the last four years, and which previously caused nightly friction at home – his anxiety gradually lessened. At the same time, Mrs Fraser asked his mother to stop trying to make him read at home. She explained that the way to help Matthew would be to read plenty of books to him, but not to make him read them himself. On the other hand word games such as Word Bingo, Junior Scrabble or Word Lotto would be well within Matthew's ability, and could make an enjoyable evening for the family. Over the next year Matthew made slow but steady progress, though he remained a rather tense, nervous child; by the time he reached comprehensive school he was still a bit backward with reading, but was able to cope quite well with a little further help in a remedial group.

The year after Matthew left a psychology graduate joined the staff of his junior school, and told Mrs Fraser that Matthew was a good example of the Yerkes–Dobson Effect. Mrs Fraser felt like telling him to watch his language, but instead asked him to explain himself in plain English. "When you're a bit anxious, such as just before an exam," he explained, "your performance tends to be better than it would be normally; when you are severely anxious, you become paralysed with anxiety, and become unable to do anything. That's how you described Matthew with his reading. When I was doing psychology at university I only heard about this in relation to rats in mazes when experimenters gave them an electric shock; I never expected to get such a nice example of it in a J3 boy!"

Questions

1 Do you believe that anxiousness can be inherited from a parent? Or is it just that the child behaves in the same way that he sees his parent behave?

2 Is it possible that praise and attention increased Matthew's anxiety after he had done a good piece of work?

3 What do you think about Mrs Fraser spending half an hour teaching Matthew about the final "e"?

4 What else would you like to know about Matthew's interest in drawing and drama?

5 What do you think Matthew feels about his younger brother? How can we explain the apparent inconsistencies?

6 What are your views about parents helping children to read at home? Are teachers too reluctant to advise parents about how they may help their children at home?

7 How can parents and teachers help a child who is being dominated by a more intelligent and more extroverted younger brother or sister?

8 If there is a choice, would you place brothers in the same class? Would you discuss the decision with the parents?

9 Would horizontal grouping have been preferable for Matthew?

10 How might Matthew have reacted if he had been temperamentally a more outgoing child?

11 Do you agree with Mrs Fraser's solution for helping Matthew? What else might she have done?

12 What difficulties might Matthew face at a comprehensive school? How could the primary school prepare for his transfer? Is there a danger in primary school teachers passing on too much information to the secondary school?

13 Can you think of other examples of the Yerkes–Dobson effect?

Anne

Main points

1 Handwriting problems can be as handicapping as backwardness in reading.

2 Homework can be more of a burden than teachers realise.

3 Too much help can hinder a child's progress.

"Anne Fletcher brought me a letter from her parents this morning. They want to come up to school and talk about her handwriting. They seem to think it's pretty bad, and that we're not doing enough about it! Have a word with her teachers will you, and find out the general opinion about her writing, and the rest of her work as well." Mr Morris, head of Crossroads Comprehensive School was waving the letter from Anne's parents rather irritably as he spoke to her year tutor. Having successfully resisted pressure from a group of vocal parents a few weeks earlier to establish a parent–teacher association in his school, he was sensitive to criticism, whether implicit or explicit.

The year tutor had never met Anne; indeed he wasn't sure that he would have known the answer if the head had asked what year Anne was in. Fortunately her parents had been considerate enough to put her date of birth on their letter to Mr Morris; but as the head doubtless recognised, this implied that they might be articulate and well-informed. It would be as well to do his homework thoroughly.

Anne's teachers turned out to be in complete agreement with her parents that her writing was poor. Not only was she painfully slow, but she was untidy and inaccurate as well. She didn't do badly in spelling tests, but made frequent errors in her free writing and when copying from a book or the blackboard. In PE she was "a tangle of arms and legs", a badly co-ordinated girl who tried hard but had no natural ability. She could not even catch a ball thrown from five yards. On the other hand, she showed remarkable aptitude in physics and chemistry. "The most promising pupil, boy or girl, in her set", her teacher wrote on the form that was circulated to all staff. Her maths teacher, too, was more than satisfied. "She would benefit from an 'A' stream", he wrote provocatively. (The school had abolished setting in maths at the end of the previous year, thus splitting the department down the middle into factions for and against.) In personality Anne was regarded by her teachers as a conscientious, studious girl who tended to take herself too seriously. She was teased by other children, who called her "swot", but as she didn't seem to mind this their teasing was mainly goodnatured. She had a nice sense of humour too, which she used unexpectedly at times when other children seemed to be getting bored. Anne had two or three close friends, but was tolerated rather than liked by the majority of her class.

Before her parents arrived, the year tutor asked the head of Crossroads school remedial department to have a look at Anne. Because many other children wrote even more slowly and less tidily than Anne did, and because her work was of a good standard in other respects, no one had thought of her as suitable for the "slow learners" group, as Patrick Henson's remedial department was still known to many staff, to his unconcealed disgust. He agreed to see Anne without hesitation. He thought she sounded interesting, and was keen to help her if he could. He had another motive too; despite a great deal of effort he had still not succeeded in persuading the head and other senior staff at the school that his department should not be regarded merely as a convenient place for the "non-academic" children – a euphemism which concealed a policy of quietly (and of course humanely) dismissing into an educational backwater children who would not be able to take exams. His arguments that bright children who were under-achieving in some respects could also benefit from an active remedial department had fallen on deaf ears. However, if the head was going to be embarrassed by pressure from Mr and Mrs Fletcher he might be able to accept Anne on his own terms, thus setting a useful precedent.

Patrick Henson was not disappointed when he saw Anne. Her writing was indeed agonisingly slow. In a timed test over five minutes Anne averaged only twelve words a minute, compared with twenty to twenty-five for most children of her age. Moreover, her whole approach to writing was making the problem worse. She was lefthanded, and covered up what she had just written with her hand as she progressed across the page; because she wrote so slowly, she continually needed to remove her hand to look at the last word, thus making herself slower still. Anne gripped the pen as though her life depended on it, and pressed so hard that the writing was clearly visible through five sheets of carbon. Anxiety was evident in the way she held her breath when writing, and bit her upper lip. Patrick wrote the head a brief report saying that Anne's teachers were certainly correct in thinking she needed help. She would become increasingly handicapped as she grew older, and this would inevitably affect her examination prospects. He thought that some progress was possible, though, and if the head and her parents were agreeable would like to see her for fifteen minutes each day for remedial writing.

Mr Morris was not altogether pleased by his colleagues' reports; he felt they demonstrated that the school had been less than alert to Anne's writing problems, and this gave him a weak hand for his interview with her parents. He comforted himself with the thought that her middle school had mentioned no problems when she transferred the previous year at the age of twelve.

He found Mr Fletcher a prickly character, but took more easily to Anne's mother. Mr Fletcher started by complaining that he had asked for help in the junior school but they had told him she was making good progress, and that her writing would get better in time. After a year and a half at Crossroads the problem seemed to be getting worse, not better. It was not for lack of practice, as she frequently took home work she had not been able to finish in class time, and sometimes spent over three hours on her homework.

At this stage Mr Morris's anxiety about criticism from Anne's parents was replaced by anxiety about Anne herself. "Whose work does she take home?" he asked, "And why does she spend so long on her homework? Children of her year shouldn't be spending more than half an hour on it." Mr and Mrs Fletcher quickly explained that they accepted that Anne's teachers could not know about all this. Whenever she got behind with her history or geography notes she borrowed another child's book and took them home to copy. The homework subjects which took her so long were English, history and religious education, which all required writing. The trouble, Mr Morris realised, was that Anne was over-conscientious, and that her own anxieties were being increased by her parents'.

At this stage he suggested to the Fletchers that Mr Henson might be able to help. Patrick listened attentively, and agreed that it was a pity the junior school had not warned them of Anne's writing problem. When asked for his opinion he said that Anne was clearly an intelligent girl whose coordination difficulties not only made her clumsy but also caused her handwriting problems. He suggested that she should be allowed to copy notes on the school's photocopying machine whenever she got behind in class, and this should also apply to homework. He asked the Fletchers to limit her homework strictly to half an hour an evening, plus ten-minutes special writing exercises, which he would give her. Meanwhile she would spend fifteen minutes a day working on the scheme he would prepare for her. At first she would have to learn not to hold the pen so tightly; this would help her to learn not to press so hard, and make it possible for her to acquire the smooth, easy hand movements necessary in writing. He proposed to teach her a more angular script than most of the other children used, since she had most difficulty with the rounded letters. If Anne had not made progress after three months on this programme, then they could discuss whether she might find typing easier than writing.

Mr and Mrs Fletcher left, satisfied that something was now being done to help Anne. Mr Morris was satisfied that a potentially troublesome interview had passed off satisfactorily. Patrick Henson, too, was satisfied at establishing a precedent which could lead to an extension of the remedial department's scope. No one asked Anne what she thought about it all.

Questions

1 Why might Mr Morris have resisted pressure to form a parent–teacher association in his school? What are the advantages and disadvantages (for parents as well as teachers) of parent–teacher associations?

2 As a parent, what would your attitude be if your child's head teacher refused to contemplate a p.t.a.?

3 How closely should a p.t.a. involve itself in the running of the school?

4 Is it logical to abolish streaming, but retain "setting" in subjects such as maths and English? At what age does ability grouping become inevitable?

5 How do you distinguish between a remedial group and a slow-learners group? How could Patrick Henson have got the difference over to his colleagues?

6 What do you think of Patrick Henson's motives in wanting to help Anne? Can political manoeuvring ("the art of the possible") be justified, or avoided?

7 Who could Anne's middle school have consulted for advice on how to help her?

8 If a parent is worried about his child's progress and feels he is getting insufficient help from the school, to whom can he turn?

9 How much homework is it reasonable to expect from secondary school children? What guidance should schools give parents about this?

10 What problems could arise from Anne being allowed to use the photocopying machine?

11 Have you any criticisms of the remedial programme which Patrick Henson produced for Anne?

12 Should the school have asked for any medical investigation?

13 At what stage could the proposals have been discussed with Anne?

14 If Anne's handwriting does not improve, can the school do anything to ensure that she is not penalised in external examinations?

Martin

Main points

1 Children fail to make progress for many different reasons. Sometimes a child is mistakenly regarded as dull when minor physical problems have caused his backwardness.

2 Even when a child has a physical handicap which is likely to affect his learning, his success in coping with this handicap depends largely on the help he gets from his parents and teachers.

At the end of his second year at a middle school in the centre of the city, Martin Simmonds was still definitely the odd man out in his class. "There are times when I really do wonder if he is all there," said Mrs Black his class teacher. "He takes so long to explain anything, that by the time he's finished I've usually forgotten the start, and he's making virtually no progress with his reading." "The thing that I notice most about him," said the PE teacher, is that he is so clumsy, and somehow he's also got an effeminate look about him."

When Martin came to Lincs School from his infant school, the infant school head teacher had written to say that he was very backward and would probably need special schooling. Since then two non-verbal intelligence tests had shown him to be of around average intelligence. The other children in Mrs Black's class were mostly sympathetic towards him; they accepted that he could not do PE very well, and on the whole they listened patiently to his laborious attempts to explain things. Sometimes, however, they got impatient and would interrupt, and when this happened Martin would give a resigned smile and fade back into the corner of the classroom. He had one or two friends, but seldom took the initiative in anything.

His educational and medical record cards showed that he had missed six months in his first year at school through pneumonia. This had since cleared up without lasting effects. There was a letter from a paediatrician at a local hospital stating he suffered from specific language retardation. At the end of his first school year his class teacher had noted on the educational record card that although he seemed a very retarded child he could use quite long sentences if anyone had the time to listen. She had also described him as a fastidious, over-careful child who could not bear a mess.

One of the dinner ladies lived in the same street as the Simmonds family. "His father's an extrovert, wiry little man with tons of energy," she told Mrs Black. "He's the 'life and soul of the party' sort of person, and he's crazy about Rugby League. Mrs Simmonds strikes me as rather a tired woman – not much energy, and quite different from her husband." A fortnight later Mrs Black met Mr and Mrs Simmonds at the end of term open evening which the school always arranged at the end of the school year. She found the dinner lady had described Mr Simmonds reliably. "Can you make the little monkey do anything?" he demanded. "I've taken him out hiking on Sundays, he's been with me to the League, and I've even tried to get him into my pub's under twelve football team; but whatever I try he's just not interested!" Mrs Simmonds smiled resignedly while her husband talked. Martin was fine with her, it appeared, but she was worried that he still could not read.

The next day Mrs Black and the PE teacher didn't know whether to laugh or cry as they talked about the visit of Martin's parents. "The poor kid's just got to look at a football rolling towards him and he falls over in a tangle of arms and legs! Do you think his father was having you on?" the PE teacher asked. Mrs Black wished she could think that, but was sure he had been serious. Nevertheless the interview did shed valuable light on Martin's behaviour. All the teachers agreed that he was naturally a clumsy child who lacked the physical coordination for the rough games most boys enjoy. He was simply unable to live up to his father's stereotype of what a boy should be like. As a result he seemed to be exaggerating the differences between himself and his father's ideal; he had gradually become fastidious, careful about his appearance and delicate in his mannerisms. Some teachers, mainly the men, thought him rather effeminate, but Mrs Black wondered whether all this was not just his way of avoiding the need to try to live up to his father's expectations. Perhaps also, his father's unrealistic expectations had driven him closer to his mother, so that he was coming to identify with the female role rather than the male one.

At the beginning of the next term Martin's head teacher asked the school medical officer to see him on her monthly visits. The doctor tested his physical coordination and control, and found that although his fine movements (such as those required in craft work, drawing and so on) were well up to the average for his age, he could not cope with gross motor movements (such as those involved in games and PE). The trouble seemed to be in the coordination of both limbs more than in any special difficulty with either limb. Martin's teachers had already recognised this, but the next thing the doctor said came as something of a bombshell. She was, she said, going to arrange an audiogram for Martin as she suspected he was deaf in his left ear. "And he sits with his right ear to the wall!" Mrs Black exclaimed in horror. In fact, Martin turned out to have only a slight hearing loss in his left ear. Provided he sat at the front of the class with his right ear closest to the teacher he would have no difficulty; nevertheless, slight though his hearing problem was, it could have contributed to his educational backwardness.

In the following months Martin's teachers made determined efforts to involve him with activities in which he might achieve a degree of success. The teacher who was organising the school's Christmas play inveigled him into helping her paint the scenery. Another teacher persuaded him to join a lunchtime chess club, and to the surprise of them both he quickly found his way into the school team. Swimming was another thing in which he developed an unexpected interest. In an attempt to help him with his reading, he was placed in a group of four children who had three sessions a week with one of the authority's peripatetic remedial teachers.

Gradually, Martin came to be accepted in his own right instead of being tolerated as the odd man out. By the time he transferred to a comprehensive school two years later he had a reading age of eight, and although the staff still thought of him as a rather vague and detached boy they no longer felt so pessimistic about his chances of survival in the secondary setting.

Questions

1 How reliable are group intelligence tests? What are their advantages and their dangers? Would you like to use them in your class? How else might you assess the ability of children in your class?

2 How might Martin's infant school teachers have recognised that he was not dull? What systematic procedures might they have adopted (apart from formal testing) which should have alerted them to his potential ability?

3 What sort of picture do you get of Martin from the second paragraph? How has this contributed towards the problem worrying his class teacher?

4 What are the possible long-term effects of a child missing six months of his first school year with pneumonia? Are some children more likely to suffer long-term educational effects than others? Does temperament come into this?

5 If a letter from a paediatrician said that one of the children in your class was suffering from specific language retardation, what further investigations would you request? Who would you ask for help?

6 When given the chance Martin could use quite long and well-constructed sentences; what does this suggest about the nature of his language problems?

7 How genuine is Mr Simmonds's concern about Martin?

8 Do you agree that Martin was "exaggerating the differences between himself and his father's ideal"? What other explanations are there for his fastidious manner?

9 Can you think of other children who have reacted to a teacher's or parent's expectations in a similar way to Martin?

10 What do you think about the school's decision to refer Martin to the school medical officer? Which other services might have been able to help?

11 How might Martin's partial deafness have affected his social and academic performance at school?

12 What are the probable reasons for

Martin's educational backwardness? What are the relative contributions of his physical problems, his mother's and father's expectations, and his two schools? Which do you think is most important?

13 Would you have selected swimming, painting stage scenery and chess as suitable activities for Martin?

14 What is the outlook for Martin at a comprehensive school?

Marian

Main points

1 "Handicapped" children are not a race apart; they have many of the same educational needs as normal children, and can often best be catered for in a normal school.

2 If a child is expected to perform at too high a level at home, she may be unable to maintain this level at school; the reverse is also true.

3 The cooperation of parents is a *sine qua non* for any educational innovation.

"She's a nice little thing really, but it's not right for her to be here." "Yes, she needs a place where they can look after kids like her. My David was telling me only last night that Miss Howard's always having to tell her again. I mean, it can't be right for the others, can it, when one like that takes all the – ." The two mothers broke off abruptly when they saw Miss Howard approaching and she again noticed the look of furtive resentment which at first she had sensed rather than seen, but which had recently been more explicit. It was nothing she had been able to put her finger on, but gradually mothers who were normally cheerful and talkative when collecting their children from school had become less open, and more protective about their children. There had been more questions about progress in reading and number, and they had been asked in a more hostile way.

Miss Howard's suspicion that Marian Hughes was the source of the friction hardened into certainty the next day when yet another mother started to complain about little Johnny's reading, and had added, slightly shamefacedly, "It must be difficult for you now, love, having to look after Marian as well as teach all the rest of them." With great difficulty Miss Howard bit back the cutting reply she wanted to make, which was that she sometimes thought Marian was as bright as little Johnny. The difference between them was that Johnny was lazy, unimaginative and dull, but looked like a normal child, while Marian had a rare congenital abnormality and was microcephalic. Yet small head or not, it was undeniable that on the infrequent occasions when she settled down to something without pressure from Miss Howard she had proved herself able to add and take away as well as at least two other children in the class. All the same her

15

presence did create problems. She seldom played with other children, unlike all the six-year-olds in her class who learnt almost as much from each other as they did from Miss Howard.

Marian's speech was intelligible but unclear, and she seldom seemed to try to make herself understood. Without personal attention she would just sit at her desk, often with her tongue lolling out, playing in an undirected, aimless way with anything that happened to be within easy reach. In the playground the big fourth-year girls tended to mother her, a form of protection and attention with which she was completely happy. Some of the boys had once upset her by chanting "pin head" in a circle around her at the far end of the playground. They had scattered when they saw an irate dinner lady bearing down on them, but the probable ringleaders were sent to Miss Peace, the headmistress, who sent them away fifteen minutes later feeling thoroughly chastened. Normally, though, Marian was a placid child, who seldom laughed or cried.

Miss Peace had been asked to take Marian into the part-time nursery when she was four. Her parents had put her name down at the earliest possible date and after checking with the Hughes's family doctor that he had no objection, she had no hesitation in offering Marian a place. "Of course, we realise that she may have to go to a special school sometime," Mrs Hughes explained, "but we'd like her to mix with normal children as much as possible first." In the nursery Marian had been an isolated little girl, apparently unable to play normally with other children unless an adult took the initiative. One of the assistants thought she was just lazy, and this impression was heightened by hearing her talk to her mother or father when they came to collect her; with them her speech was clearer, and the structure of her language less retarded. On the other hand, she never greeted them with enthusiasm when they collected her, which was strange as she *did* show some animation when greeting the teacher at the start of each session.

After a year in the nursery, the question of Marian's transfer to the infants when she reached compulsory school age came up. She had been on the local authority's "at risk" register since birth, and went to the hospital twice a year for a routine examination. At one of these she had seen a psychologist who carried out an intellectual assessment. His report was cautiously optimistic; Marian's eye–hand coordination was very retarded, and she also had great difficulty with any test requiring visual discrimination such as doing a simple jigsaw, or spotting the missing parts in pictures. On the other hand her verbal comprehension was much less retarded, and despite her unclear speech she was able to express herself quite adequately when she wanted to. "Another point which may be relevant in assessing her long term needs", the report went on, "is her parents' determination that she should live an entirely normal life; while they must certainly take much of the credit for her very high performance level compared with most similarly microcephalic children this may cause problems in the future." The report ended, unhelpfully, with a recommendation that great care be given to the question of school placement when she reached school age; although she had an IQ of 75, he was not sure what sort of school would be best for her.

Miss Peace was aware of the Hughes's ambitions for Marian. They were professional people (he was a lawyer and she had been an architect with the county council until Marian's birth), and it had taken them a long time to get over the shock of a mentally handicapped child. They were not helped by a junior doctor at the hospital who told them that Marian would be a vegetable, and that most such children died before the end of adolescence. It was not until a year and a half later that they learnt that the doctor had been twenty years out of date, and that with the development of antibiotics and other treatments Marian might well live to middle age or beyond. By this time, though, their initial despair was already changing into a grim determination to prove the doctors wrong and make Marian into an independent person.

Having discovered that Miss Howard would be pleased to have Marian as long as she could be kept under review by the local educational psychologist, Miss Peace had agreed to her parents' request that she should enter the infant school in the normal way. She was not, however, surprised when her colleague reported the latest difficulties with Marian. "There are two problems, really," Miss Howard explained. "First there's the anxiety and resentment Marian's presence is causing among parents; I don't feel much sympathy for them myself, but it's going to have an effect on the other children. Then there's the problem of Marian herself; 1 can't help feeling that she's pushed so hard at home, that she just drifts whenever that pressure is removed. The trouble is that I either have to let her drift, or give her some of the attention I should be sharing out amongst the rest."

After some discussion Miss Peace decided to ask the educational psychologist to visit the school again to discuss Marian's future with her teachers and her parents. He had already mentioned the possibility of a special school for ESN(M)* children but had been happy for her to stay where she was as long as she continued to make progress. However, when he came a fortnight later he had another suggestion. "Miss Howard is a good teacher for Marian, and it's the Education Committee's policy to integrate handicapped children into the mainstream of education. If you had two handicapped children in your school the authority could provide one fulltime child care assistant (i.e. unqualified helper) to assist their teachers. I know of a physically handicapped child in your catchment area who will reach school age next term; what do you think about it?" Miss

* A school designated ESN(M) is for educationally subnormal children with a moderate, mild degree of mental handicap, as opposed to ESN(S), which is for children with severe mental handicap.

Peace was enthusiastic; she thought that a CCA working under the direction of experienced teachers should be able to make real progress with the two children, and she could see the rest of the children benefiting as well. Miss Howard was more cautious: "It's a good idea," she said, "but I'm worried about the other mothers. We've got to win them round if it's going to work." Miss Peace replied that they were only worried because they had never discovered that physically and mentally handicapped people are not a race apart. "People are frightened of what they don't know; we must take them into our confidence."

After talking to Marian's parents and to the parents of the physically handicapped child, Miss Peace and Miss Howard arranged to meet some of the other mums, and brought their fears and resentments into the open, explaining at the same time that the school was to get another child care assistant. In addition, the psychologist met Mr and Mrs Hughes to discuss what they should regard as realistic objectives for Marian, and how they and the school could work together. It was agreed that progress should be reviewed at least twice a year.

Questions

1 Miss Howard gradually became aware of an undercurrent of discontent amongst the parents. Have you ever noticed similar undercurrents?

2 Why do you think other children's parents were so worried by Marian's presence in the class?

3 Who would you expect to be more disturbed by Marian's presence – the other children or their parents?

4 What explanation would you give other children in the school when they asked why Marian looked different?

5 What would you have done about the boys who chanted "pin head" at Marian in the playground?

6 Would you describe Marian as lazy?

7 If you were Marian's teacher, what sort of things would you particularly encourage her to do in the classroom after reading the psychologist's report?

8 If you were in Miss Peace's place, would you have agreed to take Marian?

9 Is it desirable to try to integrate handicapped children in normal schools? What are the dangers? Do you think they can be overcome?

10 Are there any educational advantages (in the broadest sense) for normal children in having handicapped children in the school?

11 How would you handle the meeting with the other parents?

12 Do you agree with the arrangements being made for Marian, or do you think it would be better for her to go to a special school immediately?

13 How long do you think Marian might be able to remain at a normal primary school?

14 Do you agree with Miss Howard's suggestion that Marian was drifting whenever the pressure from home was removed?

15 Have you ever known other children "drift" in school when the pressure from their parents is removed? Have you known other children who behave badly at home (or just "drift") when the pressure from their teachers is removed?

Tommy

Main points

1 Children who refuse to talk do not always have speech problems.

2 Tests are often unnecessary and inappropriate when assessing a child's abilities.

3 Having a large class does not make it impossible for a teacher to give a child some individual attention.

"The thing I enjoy about teaching," said Kathy Marshall with a hint of exasperation in her voice that belied her words, "is that no two children are ever alike. I spend one half of my time trying to make Jenny Whitfield shut up, and the other half trying to make Tommy Whitfield talk! The rest just have to muddle along as best they can!"

Tommy was already halfway through his second term at school. He had not gone to the nursery school because his mother had not put his name down on the waiting list until it was too late. He had never struck his teacher as bewildered by the noise and bustle of the busy reception class, but she had never been able to get more than "yes" or "no" out of him since he had been in school. What made it puzzling was that she knew he *could* talk; watching him in assembly she noticed him singing the words effortlessly, and had once heard him too, when she approached him from behind without him realising. Whenever he noticed her watching him, though, he clammed up and wouldn't open his mouth for the rest of the morning. He spoke to other children, but never when she was in earshot; she had to deduce this for herself by watching him carefully in the playground. He usually answered "yes" or "no" to a direct question, but sometimes he only nodded or shook his head. Once she had tried to make him talk by telling him to say what he wanted. She knew perfectly well that he wanted to go to the toilet, and thought he would say so. The experiment was not a success; Tommy's big, round sad eyes never blinked as he gazed fixedly at nothing in particular, and wet himself. His sister, Jenny, a noisy, extrovert little nuisance, had been full of helpful advice, explaining that you could never make Tommy do something he didn't want to. "He'll tell me, but he won't talk to anyone else," she had added provokingly.

Kathy wondered whether Tommy was educationally subnormal. She was only in her second year of teaching and had never come across an ESN child. But nor had she come across anyone like Tommy. Apart from his refusal to talk, the thing that bothered her most was that she could never meet his eye. She could not really tell whether he was listening because he would never look at her when she spoke to him. The head, who had taken the class for a week while she was ill, had been equally puzzled by this, and had written to the school's educational psychologist for advice. He was due to visit in a fortnight's time, a month after the head had written to him. Kathy Marshall, however, had mixed feelings about his visit; she had heard little about psychologists in her training and had not met any since she started teaching, but what little she had heard was bad! She was sure Tommy would refuse to cooperate in an IQ test, and as a result the psychologist would not see the other side of him. The other side was not much in evidence, but she was sure he *could* talk as long as he wasn't being watched. In addition, he was musical – she had heard him humming Beethoven's Fifth Symphony the day after it had been played in assembly – and he knew where everything was kept in her stock cupboard.

Before writing to the psychologist, the head had asked Mrs Whitfield to come early to collect Tommy from school to discuss his problems. Tommy's mother was forthcoming but unhelpful. Her son was, she claimed, "short tongued", and this made it difficult for him to say certain letters. The hospital had told her he would grow out of it; there was nothing anyone could do until he did. When the head mentioned Tommy's speech she said: "Oh no, he won't talk to you!" with a quite unmistakable note of pride in her voice. "Our Tommy's like me; keeps everything to himself, and then just blows up once in a while." As she was going out she added: "You know, I could never get on at school either!"

To Kathy Marshall's surprise, the psychologist showed no inclination to give Tommy an IQ test. Instead, he listened to everything she could tell him while the children were in assembly, and then watched Tommy in the classroom until the mid-morning playtime. As the children were going out, he asked her to keep Tommy back, and picking up a cuddly cloth dachshund that he had been playing with earlier, made the dog "bite" him on the arm. He held the dog with his arm stretched out sideways and looked out of the window on the far side of the room as he did this. Tommy gave a cautious grin, which became a giggle and then a squeal of delight when the dog "attacked" him four or five more times. "Look at Freddie, Tommy," said the psychologist, "he's coming to play with you." Each time, he only let Freddie attack when the little boy looked at him. Gradually, the psychologist held Freddie closer to his body and brought his own gaze closer to Tommy's. Each time the "attack" occurred the moment Tommy looked at the dachshund. After ten minutes the psychologist was holding Freddie in front of his own face, so that Tommy was making eye contact with him as well as with Freddie. He then passed the dog to Kathy, whispering to her to start with it at arm's length, and work towards her body. By the end of playtime she found for the first time that she was getting eye contact with Tommy.

A student was taking the class after play, so Kathy, the head and the psychologist were able to discuss Tommy. "What you were doing just now was all very well," Kathy said, "but how can I do that with a class of thirty-eight infants?" "There's no problem while we've got this student," the head countered, "and after that you could always have him for ten minutes in assembly. You never look as if you're enjoying it anyway!" (This was true; Kathy was an agnostic, and resented having to attend assembly.) As a first step, Kathy agreed to make a list of things Tommy liked doing, and use these to encourage him to talk and to make normal eye contact. Just as Freddie had only "attacked" when Tommy looked at him, so she would gradually expect more of him before letting him do the things he enjoyed. She was warned to expect progress to be slow; this would only work if the stages were so small that plenty of success and "reinforcement" were guaranteed. A further decision was to move Tommy into the parallel class, away from his sister so that he would no longer have to cope with loudly expressed expectations of what he could and could not do.

Questions

1 Is it a danger sign if one member of a family is excessively talkative and another excessively withdrawn? What preliminary questions would you want to ask?

2 Should nursery schools admit children on the basis of a waiting list, or should they admit strictly on the basis of need? How can "need" be assessed?

3 How might a nursery school have helped Tommy?

4 What are the advantages and disadvantages in placing a brother and sister in the same class? How can an infant school head teacher reach an informed decision about this?

5 How would you have coped with Jenny's "helpful advice" when Tommy wet himself?

6 Kathy Marshall had never come across an ESN child. How much time should be given to the exceptional child in teacher training? Should it be com-

pulsory for probationer teachers to visit special schools?

7 Does it matter that a child (or adult) will not make eye contact? How does this affect his interaction with other people?

8 What should schools expect of educational psychologists? What do they expect of them? Was Kathy Marshall atypical in her expectations?

9 Do colleges of education give their students sufficient information about the supporting services?

10 Did the head's interview with Mrs Whitfield throw any light on Tommy's interactions with other people? Why might the "unmistakable note of pride" have been in her voice?

11 What learning theory principles was the psychologist using in obtaining eye contact with Tommy? What other methods might he have used?

12 Does the first part of the case history

suggest any reason why withdrawing Tommy from assembly might not be a good idea?

13 Is it important for teachers to attend assembly?

14 Could the school or the psychologist have done anything to alter Mrs Whitfield's attitude towards Tommy? Could they have asked anyone else for help?

Clive

Main points

1 Sixth-formers sometimes need "remedial" help and are able to benefit from it.

2 A specific learning difficulty can cause teachers to underestimate an adolescent's ability.

"Clive has worked conscientiously throughout the year, and I expect him to get a good 'O' level in maths. However, I am not at all sure that it would be in his interest to transfer to the grammar school next term. If he leaves school now he will have no difficulty in securing one of the electrical apprenticeships with day release, despite the strong competition that exists for them. I am frankly uncertain of his ability to take maths and physics at 'A' level, and even if he does manage these I feel certain that he could not stand the pace at university. If he leaves school with no 'A' levels, or even with two poor ones, he could find himself with less openings in his chosen career of electrical engineering than he has now." *E. K. Jones, maths teacher and class teacher.*

"Clive is a very likeable boy who always tries his best. He may get a Grade II CSE in English, though this may be a little optimistic. His reading is still painfully slow, and although there are few words which completely baffle him, it takes him twice as long as anyone else in the class to read the simplest passage. Even in science subjects this will inevitably prove an immense handicap, and I really cannot see him coping with a university course." *D. R. Tennal, English teacher and head of year.*

The head of Lowtown Secondary Modern School had asked Clive Robinson's teachers for their views on whether he should apply to transfer to the local grammar school, or leave at the end of term after taking "O" levels in maths, physics, chemistry and technical drawing. In a way, Clive was one of the school's star pupils; he was more likely to obtain his four "O" levels than any of the other five pupils who were taking this number, and had shown an unusual ability with anything electrical. He was the leading member of Mr Jones's electrical club, and earlier in the year had helped him design an automatic noughts and crosses machine which was guaranteed never to lose. Unfortunately his abilities were restricted to maths and science. His English, said Mr Tennal privately, was a disaster area. His spelling was poor, though not so bad as to make his work illegible, and his writing was slow and untidy. None of this would have mattered too much if reading had not always been such a problem for him. If he had lived in a different part of the town, his parents might have had him diagnosed as dyslexic and got him into a grammar school after a lot of specialised teaching. As it was, he had arrived at Lowtown Secondary Modern School with a reading age of six and a half and an enigmatic note on his educational record card saying "Likeable boy; works well in most subjects, but determined that he'll never be able to read".

In his first year at the school Clive had done little except prove the accuracy of his previous head's summary. In his second year he joined the electrical club and immediately became a valued member. This led to an interest in science generally, in which he showed considerable ability. He discovered, for the first time, that reading had a use: you had to read to follow the instructions in kits and service manuals. The remedial teacher had capitalised on this interest, and by the end of his third year Clive was reading as accurately as most eleven-year-olds. The teacher decided that as he had now grasped the basic skills of reading she should concentrate on the more backward children in the first two years. Unfortunately, Clive's fluency (the speed at which he read) had not improved as much as his word recognition and his comprehension. The remedial teacher had assumed that this would improve with practice, but it turned out that she had been over-optimistic.

Early in his fourth year Clive read an article on electrical engineering, and through a friend of a friend of his uncle's secured an introduction to an electrical engineer who worked in the Town Hall. Liking what he heard about the job, he told his parents what he wanted to do, adding casually that this meant taking "A" levels, and then going on to university. Mr Robinson was a wages clerk for a local building firm. In Clive's junior school year he had become resigned to his oldest son not being academic, but had been questioning this judgment over the last two years. He himself was secretly frustrated by his own lack of opportunity, resulting from lack of proper qualifications, and he was gratified by Clive's recently announced ambition.

The school, as we have seen, was dubious. If Clive had been a calmer and more phlegmatic sort of boy they would not have been so worried, but he was thin and tense, the sort of adolescent who lives on his nerves. They feared he might crack up under the strain of having two or three times more to read as the work became more academic and less practical. Clive and his father, however, were unimpressed by these arguments. "You agree he's got a brain," countered Mr Robinson. "Surely there's something to help him with his reading." The head knew of nothing that might help a sixteen-year-old like Clive, but when his father threatened to complain to the education office he agreed to ask Miss Redding, the remedial advisory teacher, to see Clive and give her opinion.

Miss Redding spent most of her time in primary schools, and when she visited secondary schools it was to advise on the difficulties of very backward readers in the first or second year. By this time, Clive had a reading age of twelve on a word recognition test, though another test showed that his fluency was no better than most eight-year-olds. Miss Redding had never been faced with this sort of problem before, and took it as a challenge. She soon satisfied herself that he had no perceptual problems; he was not so anxious that he hindered his own progress, but he tended to re-read a lot of words, as if he doubted his ability to see them correctly first time. He was able to read only fifty words of an Agatha Christie book in a minute, compared with the 200 to 300 that Miss Redding considered acceptable for a boy of his age and ability. In her report to the head of Lowtown School and to Clive's parents she drew attention to all the problems Clive might face, but then wrote that she thought he might overcome these if he was sufficiently determined to do so. The remedial programme she wrote for Clive required him to spend forty-five minutes a day (twenty-five at school and twenty in the evenings) working exclusively on his reading. He must follow the words with the blunt end of a pencil, and he was to pace himself against a metronome, reading one line for each beat. At first the metronome would be put so that he read fifty words a minute, but when he was confident with this it should be increased at twenty-word intervals. However, he was not to go up more than one stage a fortnight. The book should be a popular novel, chosen by Clive from the school or public library.

At first Clive found this programme both boring and tiring. After twenty minutes his head and eyes ached, and his ears hummed with the monotonous tick of the metronome. Before long he found it less of a strain, though it was a month before he felt he was making any progress. By the following September his reading was still slow compared with other pupils in the grammar school lower sixth, but the problem no longer appeared insuperable.

Questions

1 If Mr Jones expects Clive to get a good "O" level, is it reasonable to doubt his ability to take maths at "A" level?

2 Clive's teachers appear not to have considered the frustration he might feel later in life at finding promotion blocked by lack of qualifications. What pressures could have led them to overlook this possibility?

3 Clive was a star pupil in the secondary modern school. Does this have any implications for his adjustment to the grammar school?

4 Does the case history imply that dyslexia is a middle-class excuse for backwardness in reading or spelling? Do you consider this implication justified?

5 What specialist investigations should

have been requested in the junior school?

6 In order to capitalise on Clive's electrical interests his remedial teacher must have had small groups. What are the advantages of different ways of organising remedial classes (e.g. twenty children fulltime, four groups of five children for 25 per cent of the week each, etc.)?

7 What system could the remedial teacher set up for checking on the progress of children leaving her department? Do schools place a high enough priority on this sort of follow-up?

8 Clive's father threatened to complain to the education office. Is there any way of safeguarding the interests of children who do not have interested or articulate parents?

9 Are there any criticisms of the way Miss Redding assessed Clive's reading?

10 Do you agree with Miss Redding's implicit recommendation that Clive should do "A" levels at the grammar school?

11 Comment on Miss Redding's remedial programme. Should this have been tried earlier?

Jane

Main points

1 Severe deprivation can make a child appear mentally handicapped if she is assessed too soon.

2 A child who is already emotionally upset may be more affected than other children when she catches minor illnesses.

3 Even in the late 1970s the "stigma" of illegitimacy can profoundly affect a parent's attitude towards a child.

Jane Dobb caused something of a sensation in her first week at Hilltop Primary School. She wasn't aggressive or uncooperative; it was just that no one could get near her physically, and when a teacher or child did get near her physically they still felt just as far away from her metaphorically. On her first day she had stumbled down the corridor to the classroom grasping her mother's hand tightly. Heather Jones, her young class teacher asked Mrs Dobb to stay, but she insisted on leaving after half an hour. As soon as her mother disappeared, Jane slid off her chair and crouched on all fours under the table. For the next few days she scuttled around the classroom on all fours, avoiding any form of interaction with the other children. When Heather Jones took her hand she looked alarmed in a distant sort of way, but allowed herself to be led to a table. She seldom spoke, and when she did her speech was more appropriate to a two- or three-year-old, full of diminutives and immature expressions, such as "me want to look at gee-gee book", and "boy draw bow-wow". She seemed to be a clumsy little girl too, for ever tripping over her own feet and bumping into other children. She could not, or would not, take any part in the radio music and mime programmes, crouching defensively in the corner of the assembly hall while all the other children were busy stamping around like elephants or pretending to be trees blown about in the wind.

On the other hand, inconsistencies were evident even in her first week at Hilltop School. When leaving with Mrs Dobb her coordination was noticeably better than it was during the day, and Heather Jones noticed that she chatted freely to her mother if she thought no one was looking. Although she had avoided taking part in any group activity, she had been willing to draw when given paper and wax crayons, and her drawings showed better coordination and a more sensitive use of colour than some other children in the class. Having noticed this, Heather Jones decided not to ask for any specialist investigations at this stage, but did request that Jane should be placed at the top of the list of reception class children to see the school medical officer (SMO) for routine medical examination. Jane had no brothers and sisters at the school, so nothing was known about her family apart from the fact that her mother looked well over forty, and she had a stepfather.

The SMO had a difficult time examining Jane, and at the end confessed to the head and to Heather Jones that she really didn't know if Jane was suffering from severe and irreversible mental retardation, or whether her behaviour was the result of gross deprivation, with the likelihood of rapid progress as she learnt to respond to a stimulating environment at school. The SMO did not think Jane had any hearing or sight problems, though she could not be certain, but she had seen no evidence that Jane's overall level of development had progressed as far as most three-year-olds. On the other hand this might be a mistaken impression caused by her anxiety in a strange situation. The doctor thought that her interview with Mrs Dobb had been more useful than her examination of Jane. Defensive and suspicious at first, she had gradually thawed, and by the end was answering every question without hesitation. Jane was born when she was forty-five; at first she had thought she was reaching the menopause, and the "shameful truth" had not dawned until it was too late to consider an abortion. Her husband, she had explained in great embarrassment, had died twelve years earlier and her two children from that marriage were already married with families of their own; in fact, Jane had two nephews and a niece in the infant school, a year or two older than herself. Jane was the result of a shortlived love affair with a soldier who was now serving overseas and had in any case always denied responsibility. The grown-up children thought it was "awful" when Jane was born, and had almost stopped calling for a year or so. They were better now, but Mrs Dobb still felt embarrassed by Jane's illegitimacy, and the feeling had not been dispersed by her marriage to a widower ten years older than she was, some eighteen months ago. Although her husband had legally adopted Jane, so that she now had his surname, he was a quiet, retiring man who preferred to be left in peace. Mrs Dobb had never allowed Jane to play in the street or to bring friends home; she had in effect been brought up in social isolation. "It wasn't that I didn't want her to play out, doctor," Mrs Dobb told the school doctor, "but you know what people are, and I was that depressed myself, I just couldn't do anything for her." Subsequent inquiries from the family's GP revealed that Mrs Dobb had been acutely depressed for over two years, indeed, on several occasions he had been on the verge of asking the Social Services Department to take Jane into care, so that her mother could receive in-patient treatment. Since her marriage, though, the depression seemed to have lifted.

Jane gradually started to talk to other children as the term progressed. Mrs Jones had decided not to make an issue of her refusal to do PE, even though a naughty and noisy little boy complained bitterly when she made him take part. By half-term, she was starting to use the climbing frame in the morning and afternoon playtimes, and was even joining in some of the PE sessions, though she still refused to get changed like the other children. Heather Jones had discovered that Jane liked to be noticed, but not too obviously; if she was praised in front of the class she would withdraw instantly, but a smile and a quiet word of praise or encouragement were clearly appreciated.

Heather thought she was making good progress with Jane, and told the SMO that she now felt fairly confident that she was not mentally handicapped in any way. Unfortunately, Jane did not turn up after half-term, and the education welfare officer's inquiry yielded the information that she was "poorly". When she did return, three weeks later, she was still coughing and sneezing and had a lot of thick catarrh. This cleared up within two or three days of her return, but she seemed to be back at square one socially and emotionally. However, this time her progress was more rapid than it had been in her first six weeks, and within a fortnight she had reached the stage she had been at just before the half-term holiday. At this stage Heather Jones had to go on a week's fulltime course, and her place was taken by a temporary supply teacher. Faced with this change Jane instantly regressed again, and had not really caught up when the term ended three weeks later. Jane's progress continued to be interrupted by illness and inability to tolerate change for the rest of the school year. At the end of the summer term Heather Jones was profoundly disappointed, and wondered whether she ought to go to a special school. Her anxiety about Jane was equalled only by the active resentment she felt towards Mrs Dobb, who, she was convinced, caused many of Jane's illnesses by her neurotic, over-protective attitude and by keeping her at home for longer than necessary.

Questions

1 Mrs Dobb insisted on leaving after half an hour on Jane's first morning in school. Would you encourage parents to stay for longer than this when their children start school?

2 The teachers' unions are not, on the whole, in favour of parental involvement in the classroom. What do you think about it?

3 How far can bizarre behaviour be allowed in the normal school classroom?

How far is it desirable to tolerate it?

4 What questions would you want to ask if a reception class child has speech difficulties when she starts school?

5 Heather Jones noticed inconsistencies in Jane's behaviour; she seemed more mature at certain times. How can a class teacher make systematic observations on a backward child? What would she hope to establish by making such observations?

6 What specialist investigations might Heather Jones have asked for? Who could the school medical officer have asked for a more detailed assessment?

7 If Jane had only been a year old, and teachers at the local school had heard about her mother's embarrassment, what could they have suggested to help her?

8 Was Mrs Jones justified in excusing Jane from PE while making one of the boys take part?

9 Why do you think Jane withdrew when she was praised in front of the class? Can you think of other examples where praise appears to be counter-productive?

10 What sort of special school would Heather Jones have had in mind for Jane? Is there any reason for thinking that transfer to a special school would solve any of Jane's problems?

11 Can you think of anything else the school could do (or arrange) to help a child like Jane?

Rose

Main points

1 If a child has learning difficulties or behaviour problems a detailed medical history is essential.

2 Group IQ tests are often extremely inaccurate.

3 Teachers can derive entirely false expectations about a child's ability from the spurious results of IQ tests.

Rose had not been a source of great anxiety to her teachers. At the age of ten and a half she was still, as she always had been, "happily blank", for most of the time. She was known to be dull, and the head had made a point at the beginning of the year of warning Mike Haslett, her class teacher fresh from college, not to expect too much of her. "We've always thought she hadn't got an awful lot up top, and the tests they did in the last term in the infants proved it. She's as well off here as anywhere, though, and her parents didn't want her to go to a special school."

In the course of the year Mike realised that Miss Wing, the head of Ladley County Junior School, was not in favour of special schools; she argued that children with problems needed to learn to live in ordinary society, and it didn't help to protect them by placing them in a cottonwool environment with a whole lot more handicapped children. She was equally reluctant to call in any of the authority's advisers, such as the educational psychologist, peripatetic reading specialist, or remedial advisory service. Her colleagues had mixed views. Some of them shared her mistrust of specialists, "especially the sort who come in and think they can give you all the answers," said one of them. Others, though, thought that Ladley Junior School was in danger of becoming as isolated and over-protective as the special schools its head teacher mistrusted so much; they also wondered, in their more cynical moments, whether she wasn't simply afraid of intruders finding out about the children with whom the school was failing.

Rose's "happy blankness" tended to isolate her from the other children. She seemed to live in a self-contained world, unaffected by unimportant things and people, such as school, the teachers and the other children.

Indeed, it was this absent-mindedness which caused the only real problem in teaching her. She had to be told something three or four times before it got through. None of the other children disliked her, but she only had two or three real friends.

Rose's medical record contained notes written when she was in her first and last terms in the infants; one said "low IQ", and the other "mentally defective". However, it was not clear how these conclusions had been reached. A group intelligence test, given to all children in their last term in the infants, had given her an IQ of 65. The infant school head had written: "It seems as if she will need to go to a special school, but she is not yet completely out of her depth and she might benefit from another year with normal children." The only other note of interest was from Rose's original school medical examination, when the doctor had written: "Mother says she gets bad catarrh, and doesn't hear very well at these times. Under Dr Wye at the Infirmary."

Mike Haslett spent much of his first term finding his feet in Ladley Junior School and getting into a routine. It was not until the start of his second term that he felt he was beginning to know the children as individuals. The school was not in a difficult area, and few of the children presented any exceptional challenges; apart from Rose, there were only two others who really puzzled or troubled him. Miss Wing suggested halfway through his second term that he make a study of a particular child; she expected this of all her probationary teachers, as part of their final training. When he suggested Rose she agreed readily. "You'll find her parents helpful too," she said, "but I think you'll find they get as frustrated as we do by her vagueness."

Mike soon found that Rose was both more complicated and more interesting than he had expected. For instance, her reading age was by no means the worst in the class; true, she was almost exactly two years retarded both in number and in reading, but this was no worse than four other children in his class. However, she could write neatly, accurately and quite quickly when she put her mind to it; the truth was that she never put her mind to it for more than three minutes at a time, and this gave the illusion that she was a very slow worker. Her paintings were as good as most of the other children's and he had once joined in as she and other children worked at a 300-piece jigsaw during a wet lunch hour. Jigsaws had never been his strong point, as the children had been quick to point out. "If Rose has an IQ of 65," he thought ruefully, "heaven help me!" As usual, though, she had drifted away from the group after a few minutes.

He wondered whether Rose was still deaf, but careful observation satisfied him that she was not. Although she often appeared not to hear, and had to be told to do something several times before reacting, she not infrequently answered questions spoken in a normal voice, and occasionally joined in a discussion in a way which proved she had heard everything that had gone before. All the same, at the next open night her mother did throw further light on her deafness. Rose had spent a fortnight in hospital during the summer holiday two years ago, for an operation on her ears. Before the operation the specialist had said the hearing loss was worse than they originally thought; it must have been getting worse for the last two or three years (since she started school, Mike thought), but the operation should clear the trouble completely. Both the audiologist and Rose's parents had been happy with the result of the operation, but Rose was still as absent-minded at home as at school. "Her younger brother calls her 'pistol'," said Rose's mother, "because you have to repeat everything three or four times, and he's got a gun that's a repeater."

With growing concern, Mike Haslett checked the dates and found that Rose's IQ of 65 had been taken in the term before her operation, when her deafness was at its worst. He also found out that her class had had three changes of teacher that year, and two the year before. There was nothing in her records about the operation, and he supposed that as this had taken place during the holidays, when she was between schools, the normal channels of communication had broken down. Yet how did all this explain the strange blank expression she so often wore now? Miss Wing, suddenly enthusiastic about Rose as she saw all this as a vindication of her decision not to consider a special school, suggested that when Rose suffered from deafness she must have found it a strain to listen; as a result, she simply shut off external noises which she could not hear properly and retreated into a world of her own. Being a temperamentally introverted, retiring girl, this was not difficult. By the time she had the operation, she had been doing this for nearly two years so that it had become a fixed habit which adults took for granted, dismissing it as "just Rose".

If all this was right, Mike reasoned, Rose had learnt to behave in this way as the result of her deafness, and now that she was no longer deaf he should be able to teach her to behave differently. He decided to tell her that he would never say anything more than twice; if she didn't react first time he would make sure he had her attention by putting his hand on her shoulder or waving it up and down in front of her eyes (as you do to see if someone is asleep) before repeating the instruction. At first the class treated this as a huge joke, and he wondered whether he was causing too much disruption by concentrating on Rose in this way. After a few days, though, they started to take it for granted, and the girls sitting next to her started to help him by attracting her attention as he did when she went into a daydream. The improvement was gradual but definite. He felt he had won towards the end of the summer term when he had to repeat an instruction, and Rose said with a poker face: "Sir, you're forgetting to wave!"

Questions

1 Can tests ever prove anything?

2 Can you think of other dangers in giving IQ tests? Are there any benefits?

3 What are the alternatives to intelligence testing? Is it fair to regard group IQ tests as a lazy teacher's alternative to careful observation?

4 Do you agree with the head teacher's attitude towards special schools? As a class teacher how would you try to make up your own mind?

5 Can you think of examples of schools (or class teachers) becoming overprotective towards the children? What causes this attitude?

6 If you taught at Ladley County Junior School and met a remedial adviser or educational psychologist on a course, would you try to encourage them to visit? How could they overcome Miss Wing's anxiety?

7 Have you come across other "happily blank" children? What were the probable explanations?

8 If a child is told to do something three or four times, what effect does this have on the other children's expectations?

9 How could the head teacher obtain a report from Dr Wye, assuming he would not send it to her directly as it would be a breach of confidentiality? Who should be responsible for ensuring that this sort of information is obtained?

10 Is it reasonable of Miss Wing to expect every probationary teacher to make a detailed study of one child? What sort of supervision is desirable in the probationary year?

11 Can reading tests have the same dangers as intelligence tests? Are they really necessary if the teacher keeps his records systematically?

12 Was Mike Haslett justified in concluding, before meeting her mother that Rose was no longer deaf?

13 What did his interview with Rose's mother suggest about the interaction between Rose and her family?

14 Do you agree with Miss Wing's explanation for Rose's "happy blankness"?

15 Would you have tackled this problem in the same way as Mike Haslett? Do you think he was justified in singling Rose out for special treatment, particularly as the other children noticed this and commented on it?

Richard

Main points

1 It is easy to attribute all a child's difficulties to family problems. Sometimes a child has a specific learning difficulty which has nothing to do with his disturbed family.

2 A tendency to problems such as obesity can be increased by stress in the family.

Richard Marsh's infant school head teacher had referred him to the child guidance clinic when he was just six. "He is an overweight little boy, and is often very aggressive with the other children;" she wrote, "his class teacher has noted that when his mother collects him in the afternoon she alternates between over-protection and extreme impatience. Richard seems resentful when he is with her, and it may be that she is the one who needs help."

Checking Richard's record five years later, his class teacher discovered that the clinic team had agreed with the infant school head. A letter from the consultant child psychiatrist to the school medical officer stated that Mrs Marsh had been in her early forties when he was born. With her first two children married and engaged she had been shocked and horrified to discover herself pregnant. She had suffered from depression for over two years after his birth, and was only now regaining her former health. Having been forced to give up a promising secretarial career, she was now planning to return to the same firm, though at a much lower level than the one she had left. The psychiatrist's letter made clear that Richard's problem should be seen as a reaction to his mother's. However, she was now recovering and the outlook was good. A brief report from the educational psychologist said that Richard was of average intelligence, and although he was not reading this was not altogether surprising in view of his age and the family disturbances. The case had been closed six months before Richard left the infant school. Mrs Marsh found it difficult to fit the interviews in with her new job, and the psychiatrist agreed with her that the job was more important.

Eric Cook, Richard's class teacher in his final year at the primary school, reflected that this was all very well, but although Richard now read fluently, his written work was still appalling. Moreover, the "overweight little boy" had now grown into an obese big boy who was not beyond using his weight to intimidate other children. He was sometimes called "tank", a name which he clearly enjoyed as much as he enjoyed charging from one end of the playground to the other, scattering everyone in his path. He could sometimes be aggressive, and was heartily disliked by some of the teachers because of this. Eric Cook, on the other hand, had a soft spot for him, and Richard never presented him with any behaviour problems. Indeed, he was often a delight to have in the class since throughout his junior school career he had excelled in oral work, and always showed a sharp sense of humour. His written work was quick, full of mistakes, and untidy. At first Eric Cook had thought it was just carelessness, but standing over Richard and making him work as slowly and carefully as possible produced no real improvement. His art work was good, but he concealed a poor sense of form behind a generous and imaginative use of colour. The poor written work, though, was already a problem and would become a real handicap when he moved up into the secondary school.

Eric's first thought was to ask the head to refer Richard back to the child guidance clinic. At first sight the psychiatrist's assessment that Richard's difficulties were caused by his mother's problems appeared consistent with his own observations. He well remembered the open day when Mrs Marsh had told him about Richard's diet. "He's very good about it;" she explained, "even when I put a second helping on his plate he still doesn't have it!" Yet a moment later she was telling him, with unmistakable bitterness in her voice, how irritating Richard was, and how he cheeked his dad by answering back and making "clever" remarks. Having read the earlier reports, it seemed clear to Eric that Mrs Marsh was compensating for her resentment towards Richard by giving him all the food he could eat, even if this did make him obese. Quite unnecessarily, she had told him about the arrangements for Richard to go to a neighbour (who gave him "a good tea with bread and cake") until she returned from work and could provide a cooked meal. He had thought she must in reality be feeling guilty about having returned to a fulltime job, and as a result was doing everything possible to persuade herself that she was not being a bad mother.

Nevertheless, Eric did not ask the head to refer Richard back to the child guidance clinic. He had a suspicion that the clinic team had looked too closely at Richard's family, and not closely enough at Richard himself. If the problem was only in the home, he reasoned, then surely Richard would be backward in everything, and not just in his written work. His suspicions were strengthened by Richard's difficulty when the children in his project group were asked to draw a map of Australia freehand, as the school's duplicating machine had broken down. While the others copied the outline without trouble, Richard's attempt was unrecognisable, and Eric Cook intervened to save him further embarrassment. He kept Richard behind at the end of the session and asked him to copy some shapes which he drew for him. To his astonishment, Richard's copies were virtually unrecognisable, the sort of attempt he would have expected from a child of six, but certainly not from an obviously intelligent eleven-year-old.

Richard knew that his copies were poor and was visibly embarrassed. Eric Cook was also embarrassed; he regarded himself, and was regarded by his senior colleagues, as an able, conscientious and experienced teacher, and yet he had never noticed something which must have been staring him in the face since the previous September. "How on earth didn't I notice that you couldn't do this sort of thing?" he asked, more of himself than Richard. "Well, sir," said the boy awkwardly, "Pete always helps me with the difficult bits, and I help him with his maths; you're always telling us to help each other if we get stuck, and I can't ask you to come and copy things for me, can I?" Eric had to agree, but couldn't help asking how Richard had learnt to write when he found copying so difficult. The reply was crushing: "You told me last week that it was time I learnt to write!"

After a discussion with the head, Eric Cook asked the part-time remedial teacher, Mrs Unwin, for help with Richard. She agreed at once, and surprised him by saying Richard had been her star pupil in his first term in the junior school, when she had got over his "blockage" about reading.

When he rejoined her group Mrs Unwin asked him to copy the four abstract figures which test eye–hand coordination in Daniels' and Diack's Standard Reading Tests. His copies were not unlike the ones given as examples in the book which, the authors claimed, show "an inability to perceive, at a level of perception high enough to direct the hand, the interrelation of the detailed parts. . . . There is little use trying to teach this child to read until his performance in this task improves". Mrs Unwin regarded the Daniels and Diack test, quite correctly, as one of the most useful tests on the market in the assessment of backward readers. It was clear, however, that poor eye–hand coordination had not stopped Richard learning to read. She told Eric Cook that she would have him four times a week for the next three months and give him an intensive course of perceptual training exercises, concentrating on eye–hand coordination. She also suggested it would be a good idea to refer him back to the child guidance clinic for a further opinion on whether they could do anything to improve the mother–child relationship.

Questions

1 If Mrs Marsh was the person who really needed help, was the infant school head right to have referred Richard to the child guidance clinic? What else might she have done?

2 The psychiatrist appears to have been

in favour of Mrs Marsh returning to work. When is it better for a mother to go out to work than to stay at home looking after the children ?

3 Teachers probably cannot stop the use of nicknames, but should they ever use them when talking to children ?

4 Richard enjoyed his nickname. If children and teachers often called him "tank", what effects might this have had ?

5 Is Eric Cook justified, on the evidence in the third paragraph, in concluding that Richard's poor written work is not due to carelessness ?

6 Do you agree with Eric Cook's conclusions about the mother–child interaction, or could he have been jumping to conclusions ?

7 Can you think of other examples where teachers (or psychologists) have looked too closely at the family, and not closely enough at the child himself ?

8 Can you think of other children who conceal a disability in the same sort of way as Richard ? How do some adults hide an inability to read ?

9 Richard could read fluently, even though the diagnostic tests suggested that he ought not to be able to. What does this suggest about the use of tests ? Can you think of other examples where they might be misleading ? Is there any way of guarding against "false" results ?

10 How would you set about improving the mother–child relationship if you were working in the child guidance clinic ?

Debra

Main points

1 Teaching methods that are suitable for one backward reader are quite unsuitable for another; remedial teachers must assess each child individually.

2 Anxiety about reading can lead to other problems which appear on the surface to be unrelated.

3 The other problems may remain, even when their original cause has been removed.

"Don't try to tell me this one isn't ESN, because I'm jolly sure she is!" Miss Hodges, the Head of High Beach Middle School glared across the table at the nervous young educational psychologist sitting opposite her. Debra was the third child Miss Hodges had referred to the psychologist with the intention that he should arrange for them to be transferred to a school for educationally subnormal children. To her unconcealed disgust, the psychologist had pronounced both the other two children to be of somewhat below average intelligence, but certainly not ESN. He had put his foot right in it with the first child, because he had said that all the boy needed was a little bit of good remedial teaching. It was only after he had said this that he discovered that Miss Hodges herself had been running the remedial class in the school since she took it over twenty-five years previously. "Did you say he had got an IQ of over 85?", she had said. "Then it must be sheer laziness that's stopping him learning. We'll soon change that!" The psychologist shuddered at the thought of Miss Hodges's remedial teaching, and shuddered again at the thought of the techniques she would undoubtedly be using to change the boy's laziness. Unfortunately she had friends in high places; she was on Christian name terms with the Chairman of the Education Committee, and also knew the Chief Education Officer well. In the circumstances all he could do was feel thankful that she had only two more years to retirement. Complaints about the school would certainly not be well received.

With a feeling that he had been through it all before, the psychologist started to carry out an intellectual assessment with Debra. As he had half expected, he found that Debra was of average intelligence; however, in the test in which Debra had to arrange sets of pictures in the right order to make a sensible story, she had arranged four of the five sets from right to left, but in the correct order. The third set she had arranged from left to right, but then looked at it hard and said, "Oh, that's wrong way, isn't it?" She then rearranged the pictures so that they went from right to left. Later, Debra's class teacher said that she had also noticed this; on two occasions when she had asked Debra to call out a list of words, she had started at the top right-hand corner and moved to the left. Analysis of Debra's errors on a reading test showed that she made an unusually large number of reversals; she still got confused between "b" and "d", and "p" and "q", and also read the word "pot" as "top" and "tip" as "pit". "I suppose it's a pity really that Debra wasn't born Chinese or Jewish," remarked her class teacher, "then her eye movements going from right to left would have been quite an asset instead of a handicap!"

For two and a half years Debra had been receiving remedial reading lessons from Miss Hodges. Miss Hodges had decided views on how remedial reading should be taught. "Back to old-fashioned phonics, that's what they need!" she used to say, and took children off the Ladybird series, which the infant school used in conjunction with Nippers, and put all her remedial children on her own highly prized system of phonic instruction. "That damned cat still sitting on the mat," said Debra's exasperated class teacher to the psychologist.

Debra herself seemed on the surface remarkably unaffected by her years of failure. She was a plump, placid girl, who seemed quite resigned to the fact that she couldn't read, and would probably never be able to. On the other hand, though, her mother had told her class teacher on open night that she had been wetting the bed for over a year and a half; also she had recently started to have nightmares, and once her mother heard her shout, "Not more reading!" On a school outing she had confided to her teacher that she wet the bed, and had admitted that this worried and embarrassed her a lot. She was terrified that the other children might find out. Her teacher knew that bed-wetting is not always a sign of anxiety in a child but does often start at times of stress. Apart from her sequencing difficulties, there was no reason at all why Debra should have had difficulty in learning to read. If these had been recognised when she was at the infant school, or even in her first year or so at her junior school, a few simple remedial exercises in left–right orientation would undoubtedly have led to her making rapid progress. As it was, she had been subjected to two and a half years exceedingly formal remedial teaching which did nothing to alleviate her confusion between left–right and right–left orientation. She was now convinced that she could not read, and was apathetic towards the idea of further help. In addition, she was suffering the embarrassment and discomfort of nocturnal enuresis.

Attempts to explain Debra's remedial needs to Miss Hodges met with stony silence. "These new-fangled methods;" she said later in the staffroom, "that child is plain dull, and lazy as well, she shouldn't be here." In a sense, Miss Hodges was quite right; Debra really would have been better-off elsewhere, even though there was no educational justification for her to be moved from a normal middle school. As it turned out, Debra's parents moved her shortly after she was seen by the psychologist, and she went to a different school. This school was also fairly formal, but the remedial teacher readily agreed to give Debra specific help with sequencing skills that would help her to acquire the smooth left–right eye movements that are required in reading English. Slowly, Debra started to make progress, and the number of letter and word reversals gradually declined. She remained enuretic though, and it was not until she was given a "buzzer"* that this cleared up. "What a pity she couldn't have been helped three years ago," remarked her new class teacher.

Questions

1 Is it a good thing for head teachers to have a regular group of children, such as a part-time remedial group?

2 Was the psychologist wise to have told Miss Hodges the child's IQ? What proportion of children would score between 85–115 on most intelligence tests?

3 Would it have helped Debra's teachers to know her IQ? How might this have confused the issue?

4 How would a good remedial teacher set about assessing a child like Debra?

5 Without writing a list of words, how could you screen a group of backward readers for sequencing difficulties?

6 Are there any backward readers who might benefit from "old-fashioned phonics"?

7 There is an assumption that Debra's bed-wetting was related to her anxiety about reading. How might you find out if this is justified?

8 What suggestions could the class teacher have made when Debra's mother told her about her bed-wetting?

9 Can you think of other children whose particular perceptual (or phonic) problems have not been treated in their remedial sessions?

10 Can you think of other children who have become apathetic (or developed overt behaviour problems) as a result of academic failure?

11 What should the psychologist have done if Debra's parents had not moved her from High Beach Middle School?

12 Could Debra's class teacher have done anything to help her if she had remained at High Beach Middle School?

13 Why might a problem (such as bed-wetting) persist after the original cause (e.g. anxiety about reading) has disappeared? Can you think of any other instances?

14 How can a teacher arrange for a child to receive treatment for bed-wetting?

15 What would you do if a child in your class was being teased about bed-wetting?

* The buzzer is a method for treating bedwetting, in which two wire gauze blankets are laid beneath the child's sheet, separated by another sheet, so that when the child starts to wet the bed a loud alarm goes off. Gradually the child starts to wake up before the alarm goes off, and in many cases treatment is successful within two months.

Peter

Main points

1 The effect children have on the behaviour of their teachers is often as great as, or greater than, the effect teachers have on the behaviour of their pupils. The main difference is that children tend to be more aware of their teacher's influence than teachers are of their pupils'.

2 What teachers and parents see as a behaviour problem may in fact be the only thing that is making life bearable for a child.

3 When teachers and parents cooperate uncritically, the result may increase the child's sense of isolation.

"Will you ask that Peter Dean why he won't wear a white shirt and tie?" The deputy head of a well-known London comprehensive school was clearly exasperated and infuriated by one of his first-year pupils when he buttonholed the counsellor on the second day of the summer term. "He's the *only* first-year boy who doesn't come to school wearing uniform; on the last day of last term he turned up wearing a T-shirt! I told him that as it was the last day of term I wasn't going to see it, but he would have to be properly dressed this term, and blow me if the little bugger doesn't turn up wearing the same thing on the first day this term!"

This history is not about school uniform. It is about the way one child is obtaining success. The facts of Peter's history were known to the school. His father had had to leave school at the age of fifteen, but by sheer hard work and determination had obtained "O" levels, "A" levels, a BA and a PhD, and was now lecturing in engineering on a polytechnic degree course. He had married shortly after obtaining his doctorate, and had five children, all but one of them highly successful by all normal standards. The oldest was well on his way to obtaining an Oxford D Phil, and the youngest had recently won a national maths competition for primary school children. Mr and Mrs Dean were both intelligent and articulate, but were also conscientious parents, anxious to do the best for all their children.

Peter, as his class teacher elegantly put it, was the nigger in the family's woodpile. His academic attainments were well below average for his age;

when he read anything, which was seldom, it was generally the most disreputable comic strip. However, he had once been caught reading *Fanny Hill* during morning assembly. He had few interests, and had truanted on several occasions. His only friends were three boys who lived in the most rundown part of the school's catchment area, and who had all been in trouble with the police. They came to the comprehensive from a different primary school but soon after the start of the second term this heavenly trio had become an equally heavenly quartet.

Baffled by Peter's refusal to cooperate, the school was slightly relieved to find that his parents were equally baffled and exasperated. Mr and Mrs Dean willingly accepted the suggestion that Peter should see the peripatetic school counsellor, who in due course discussed the problem with the teachers, his parents, and finally though not least, Peter himself. The school did not find the counsellor's suggestions useful. He pointed out that Peter was of average intelligence but was working well below potential. In a highly intelligent, ambitious family, a child who is only of average intelligence can quickly come to feel lost and undervalued. His siblings had always brought back glowing end of term reports, glittering with A's and B's; Peter brought back reports which ranged from the sympathetic to the critical, mainly consisting of C's and D's, with the occasional E. The only subjects in which he shone were art and drama, but these were subjects which were somehow not thought as important as English, arithmetic and so on.

This case history is about success. Peter's story seems to be one of failure, but is it? Peter had found at an early age that he could never achieve success through competition with his outstandingly gifted brothers and sisters. He was of average intelligence, and was too perceptive to be fooled by the kindness and sympathy which masked his parents' disappointment. When he was nine he knew that his six-year-old sister could read better than he could (she had a reading age of twelve), and he also knew that his parents were proud of her. He sensed, rightly or wrongly, that his parents' interest in his art and drama was a cover for their disappointment in his failure to shine at anything academic, or to share their intellectual and mechanical interests. For several months at the start of his last year at his primary school he had been withdrawn and morose. Towards the end of the year the depression had lifted but had been replaced by the pattern of behaviour which was worrying his comprehensive school teachers. Peter's attempts to obtain success on adults' terms had been unsuccessful; he was now obtaining it on his own terms. He could not compete with his successful brothers and sister, but he could compete on equal terms with the trouble-making trio who had joined the school at the same time that he had. He gladly accepted their offer of friendship. He quickly found new ways to win friends and influence people. For instance, by the delightfully simple device of coming to school wearing a T-shirt, he could reduce the all-powerful deputy head of a school of over 1,200 pupils to a state of quivering fury.

In discussing school with the counsellor, Peter was remarkably articulate; "They don't like me and I don't like them!" "Have you given them any reason to like you?" asked the counsellor. "When I do something good they just throw it back at me, but if there's any trouble it's always Peter Dean they look for," said Peter aggressively. "Then bring me some of this good work you're talking about." Peter did. He brought a book he had made on the history of Tottenham Hotspurs Football Club. By any standards it was a good piece of work. Neatly done, his own work, and well presented. Peter had done this as part of a homework project, in which the children had been given the task of finding out at home about a subject of their own choice. Peter's choice had been approved by his teacher. When the work was returned the only comment was the initials of the teacher. Peter also brought the books of three other children, none of them as good as his, but in all of them detailed comments had been written by the teacher.

There is hope for Peter. He still has fight in him, and he is not prepared to give up. His ways of obtaining success bring him no more happiness than they bring to his parents or to his school, but they do make life bearable. As long as this aggressive resilience remains there will be a chance of helping him to find other ways of obtaining recognition and success. The children who give up the unequal struggle, often in middle adolescence, and retreat into the indifference of despair are the ones who should most worry the consciences of teachers, parents, psychologists and social workers. Peter is a problem, certainly to his school, and probably to himself, but he has not reached this stage.

Questions

1 Is Peter's school right to place so much emphasis on correct uniform? What are the arguments for and against abolishing uniform? If the school does have uniform, should children be compelled to wear it?

2 How else might Peter's teachers have reacted when he turned up wearing a T-shirt? What might have been the effect on Peter (and on the other children) of the possible alternatives?

3 Is it likely that Peter intended to be caught reading *Fanny Hill* during morning assembly? If you had been the teacher concerned what would you have done?

4 What warning signs did Peter's primary school have that he was "at risk"?

Which of the advisory services should they have asked for help?

5 Peter's siblings had always brought back reports "glittering with A's and B's". Peter himself had reports "mainly consisting of C's and D's, with the occasional E". What is the purpose of school reports? Do they help the parent? Do they help the child? Are grades (A–E) useful, either at primary or secondary level? What are the alternatives to the traditional school report?

6 Might the school unintentionally have been reinforcing Peter's refusal to cooperate? How?

7 Peter's six-year-old sister had a Reading Age of twelve. Does this suggest anything about the priorities of her

teachers or parents? Should there be a distinction in primary schools between creative subjects and the three Rs? Can a secondary school give the same status to subjects such as art and drama as to the traditional academic subjects?

8 Peter had been morose and withdrawn at the start of his last primary school year; later the depression had lifted, but had been replaced by more outwardly troublesome behaviour. Do you accept the implication that both patterns of behaviour had the same cause? Can you think of any other children in whom one problem seems to have developed out of another?

9 From Peter's point of view, was the outwardly difficult behaviour more satisfying than the depressed, morose state from which it seemed to develop? Would it have been easier for his primary school to have helped him when he first became withdrawn? What might they have done?

10 Do you agree that Peter "was now obtaining success on his own terms"? Who was having the greater effect on the other persons's behaviour – Peter or the deputy head?

11 What did Peter's teachers expect of him? What happened when he lived up to those expectations? What happened when he did not? Explain Peter's interactions with his teachers in terms of reinforcement principles.

12 What could be done to help Peter's teachers become more aware of his qualities, and to reinforce his good work?

13 How could the school help Peter to find other ways of achieving recognition and success?

14 How much responsibility do you think the school bears for this problem? How much can the school do about it?

15 Do you agree that "there is hope for Peter"? Can you think of other children who have been labelled "maladjusted" or "disturbed" by teachers or psychiatrists when their behaviour can be viewed as a quite healthy reaction to difficult circumstances if it is looked at from a different angle?

Andrew

Main points

1 Children behave provocatively because they have learned to expect consistent reactions from their teachers. These reactions are often reinforcing for the children.

2 Smoking is an easy way to defy authority.

3 Normal schools sometimes have to help children who are considered too difficult for special schools.

"Now I've seen everything!" The note in the student's voice was not of anxiety or alarm, so much as of profound admiration. Halfway through his second teaching practice he was finding life difficult at the High School – a mixed secondary school in a small country town. At the end of the corridor, outside the vestibule leading to the head's study, Andrew Coombes, nearly fifteen, was leaning against the door frame coolly smoking a pipe. The student had heard a good deal about Andrew, but had only met him twice. The first time was when Andrew had successfully destroyed his carefully planned history lesson with a few well-chosen questions; the second was two days ago when he had found four boys smoking behind the toilets and had sent them to the head for the regulation punishment. And there was Andrew again, outside the head's study, smoking a pipe! "Thank God I haven't seen him!" muttered the student, and scuttled furtively but thankfully down a corridor on his right, feeling that the diversion was a small price to pay for avoiding this particular incident.

The next person to see Andrew did not escape so easily; it was the head himself, emerging from his office with a distinguished visitor, the deputy chairman of his governing body. Andrew casually pocketed the glowing pipe as the door opened; in fact he did it so casually that both men had ample time to take in the whole scene. Mr Ramsden wondered for an instant if he could pretend not to notice, but feeling his partner stiffen rejected the idea at once. "Take it out," he said icily, "and put it out. Then wait until I get back."

"As you see, we are not without our problems," he remarked dryly as they walked down the corridor, seething inwardly at yet another piece of blatantly provocative behaviour from Andrew Coombes. The deputy chairman of the governors was thoughtful. "That was Coombes's boy, wasn't it?" he asked as they walked on to the car park. "His father and I sit on the same committee in the chamber of commerce. We usually have a drink together afterwards. As a matter of fact, I had dinner with his parents a fortnight ago. Do you have much trouble with – ?" "Andrew," said Mr Ramsden. "Yes, I'm afraid we do. In fact, we never get much else. And to make it worse, we can't find out why; with most problem children you don't have to look for an explanation – broken home, illness or death in the family, over-anxious parents or something. But Andrew's had teachers, psychologists and psychiatrists beaten ever since he was five. He was put on probation last year but it's having no effect."

Angry and embarrassed, he returned to his office, where Andrew was waiting patiently. For Mr Ramsden not the least exasperating thing about him was his quiet, submissive, almost cringing manner, so totally out of keeping with the blatantly provocative nature of his behaviour. It was not hard, he knew from past experience, to reduce Andrew to tears, though corporal punishment seldom if ever had this effect. Mr Ramsden felt his temper rising still further as he questioned Andrew. Yes, came the reply, polite but resigned, he had been smoking; he was very sorry; he didn't know what had made him do it. He had been sent by Mr Daniels, his maths teacher, for passing a cigarette to another boy who, Andrew admitted, had not wanted it in the first place. Mr Daniels had confiscated the packet before sending Andrew to the head, but had overlooked the unused packet of tobacco in his jacket pocket. All Andrew could say after further questioning was that he might have opened the packet to steady his nerves!

Mr Ramsden was angrier than he had been for a long time. Mistrusting his own ability to act rationally he dismissed Andrew with a curt: "I'll decide what to do when I've spoken to your parents." As the boy turned, a thought struck him; "Did you know I had a visitor?" "Yes," answered Andrew, visibly shaken for the first time in the interview. "Did you know who it was?" "Yes, sir," Andrew replied, his eyes filling with tears. "That's all, I'll see you again tomorrow."

Before writing to Mr Coombes, Mr Ramsden looked up the notes on the welfare meeting at which Andrew had been discussed a month previously. All his teachers had been asked about his behaviour and progress. Comments ranged from the laconic "he disrupts my lessons more politely than any boy I have met" from his French teacher, to the equally laconic "I will be happy to attend the meeting, but my opinion of this boy cannot be committed to paper" from his science mistress. Some teachers said they did not regard him as a problem at all, but on the other hand they had to admit that they seldom noticed him – he seemed to fade into the background. The only dissenting voice was that of the art teacher, who said Andrew had ability and worked hard in his weekly lesson. There was no evidence that he got on better with men or women teachers, or with older rather than younger ones. The staff were agreed that his frequent offences were not motivated by a wish for attention from other boys; he was unpopular but seemed unworried by this. Nor did he seem to want adult attention; when taken to task he almost always seemed genuinely upset and bewildered. His politeness was his natural manner, with scarcely a trace of bravado; no one thought he enjoyed his notoriety. His probation officer had been as puzzled as his teachers; Andrew always kept his appointments punctually, but there were no signs that probation was helping him.

Mr and Mrs Coombes came to see Mr Ramsden two days later. Mr Coombes was in his early sixties. He had married late in life, on his return to England after spending over twenty years in business in a succession of Asian and African countries. His wife was only a few years younger, and had given up her own successful career in banking when Andrew was born. "He was a surprise," she had told a psychiatric social worker years earlier on Andrew's first visit to a child guidance clinic, but her tone made clear that he was in fact a bitterly regretted mistake. The interview was as successful as Mr Ramsden had expected. Mr and Mrs Coombes were embarrassed and upset. They were quite ready to agree, as Mr Ramsden had known they would be, to anything he suggested, but at the same time they successfully conveyed the impression that nothing was likely to work. He was left with an uncomfortable but clear impression of implacable hostility between parents and son.

Unfortunately, Mr Ramsden reflected after they had left, there was little he could suggest. Andrew was too old for the authority's school for maladjusted children, and three years earlier his parents had rejected the offer of a residential school because there was too little discipline. Having visited the school himself, Mr Ramsden secretly sympathised with their decision; he had been appalled by the anarchic atmosphere, and scruffy appearance of children and staff. The helping agencies had failed to help Andrew at home; the education department had failed to find a satisfactory special school; so the High School would have to soldier on until Andrew left school or committed a criminal offence serious enough to warrant removal from home. But if he was to remain on Mr Ramsden's register a way would have to be found to prevent him upsetting staff and other children. Before the next welfare meeting Mr Ramsden asked the art teacher if he was willing to have Andrew for the last hour each day. On receiving consent, he asked all his teachers to send him to the office at the least sign of provocation or disruptive behaviour. At the office Andrew would be given some work to do and sent to one of the interviewing rooms for half an hour or so until the end of the lesson, whichever was greater. The interviewing room was small and boxlike, with no outside window, and furnished only with table and chair. If Andrew was not sent to it at all by the end of the day he would be allowed to spend the last hour in the art room. The staff were unimpressed by Mr Ramsden's proposals, saying that he would have to spend over 75 per cent of every day in the "box-room", and this would prevent him doing any art at all. Reluctantly, though, they agreed to give it a try.

Questions

1 When the student caught some boys smoking he sent them for "the regulation punishment". What do you think about fixed punishments for specified offences?

2 What could the student's evasive action imply about the staffroom relationships at the High School?

3 What would you have done if you had been in the student's position when he saw Andrew smoking his pipe?

4 What would you have done if you had been in the head's position? Would you have waited until the deputy chairman of the governors left before taking any action?

5 Andrew was easily reduced to tears, but not by corporal punishment. Why might this be the case? Does it carry any implications for his management at school?

6 Do you know other children who use "dumb insolence" as effectively as Andrew? How do you deal with it?

7 If Andrew had not already been referred to any of the specialist agencies, who would you ask for help?

8 What problems commonly face an only child?

9 What problems commonly face children with elderly parents? How do you think these applied to Andrew?

10 Does "the scruffy appearance of children and staff" at the residential special school which Mr Ramsden visited necessarily mean that there would have been "an anarchic atmosphere"? Could there have been good reasons for children and staff looking scruffy?

11 What do you think of Mr Ramsden's proposals for Andrew?

12 The interviewing room sounds a pretty depressing place. Is it equally bare and depressing in your school? What should be done about it?

13 How long a trial should Mr Ramsden give his proposals before calling another case conference to review progress?

14 Can you think of any other solutions?

Maureen

Main points

1 Children learn "maladjusted" behaviour in just the same ways that they learn other forms of behaviour.

2 Attention-seeking children often have a real need for the attention they are seeking.

3 Punishment at school may have the effect of increasing the amount of attention-seeking behaviour; some children have learnt that punishment is the only way they can get attention, with the result that it has become reinforcing for them.

4 Teachers can help attention-seeking children to learn new and more constructive ways to obtain attention.

Maureen, aged eleven, was in her first term at a comprehensive school. One morning she went up to her conventional, respectable, not to say staid, history teacher and said, "Please Sir, do you believe in sex before marriage?" Sir managed with an effort to keep his voice steady, and told Maureen that if she really wanted to know she could come and see him privately. Later in the term a student on his first teaching practice found himself with Maureen's class on his first day. He was more than a bit disconcerted when Maureen walked up to him at the beginning of the lesson and announced: "Hullo, I'm Maureen and I do what I want to!" This was something which his course had not taught him to cope with, but when he discussed it with his supervisor he discovered that Maureen was more or less telling the truth. In lessons which she did not like she either ran out of class or called attention to herself in a variety of ingeniously disruptive ways. She had several times been found running round the school barefoot, often during PE lessons, and her frequent loud "accidental" burps were exquisitely timed to have the maximum disruptive effect. Other children derived a certain vicarious satisfaction and enjoyment from her exploits, but she was not really popular. She frequently used foul language to other children, in a way that seemed calculated to shock them.

The other children told her teachers to hit her; it was what they used to do at the junior school, and it was the only thing she understood! Nevertheless, they did agree that it had not stopped Maureen from showing off for more than two or three days at a time. Mr Franks, her year tutor at the comprehensive school, recognised her behaviour as attention-seeking and was reluctant to gratify, and hence encourage, Maureen's attempts to get attention by caning her, even though caning girls was still permitted at the school.

Mr Franks therefore rang up the junior school to see if they could give any confidential information which was not on Maureen's junior school report. The junior school head teacher described Maureen as a "thundering nuisance", but added that her father was epileptic and that she had been in the care of the local authority at least once. She had often come to school in a dirty, uncared-for state, and on one occasion had extensive bruising on her legs and buttocks. She told the teachers that her father had been hitting her for staying out late. Her parents were divorced and it was thought that she had little contact with her mother.

Since arriving at the comprehensive school, Maureen's physical state seemed to have improved, but her behaviour remained a headache for most of her teachers. Her father was invited to come and discuss Maureen's progress with the year tutor. However, the next day she told her class teacher that her father had punished her for being a nuisance at school. Father did not turn up to meet the year tutor, who hesitated to send him another letter in case Maureen got into further trouble. The education welfare officer was reluctant to visit the home as Maureen's attendance had been perfect, and the head teacher's policy was that the teachers themselves should not carry out home visits.

The year tutor therefore rang up the Social Services Department and was eventually put through to the social worker who had arranged the reception into care the previous year. The social worker told him that Maureen's parents had separated two years previously, after a marriage that had been unhappy since the start. Maureen's mother had eventually deserted the family, and her father had been given custody of Maureen and her younger sister by the matrimonial court. Surprisingly, the court had not placed the children on a supervision order, but when Mr Smith had been admitted to hospital following an epileptic seizure the children had been taken into care. Maureen and her sister spent a month in a children's home, by which time father had returned home and with the help of anticonvulsant drugs was apparently managing satisfactorily. He had made clear to the social worker that he wanted no further visits, and the latter felt unable to reopen the case unless the school had definite evidence of cruelty or neglect.

With this information the teachers felt that they had reached an impasse. In the circumstances, all they could do was to rely on guesswork. They knew that temperamentally Maureen was a lively, outgoing girl, and that as a younger child she would have had the normal infant's need for affection, attention and recognition. However, the information from the social worker had suggested that her parents had been wrapped up in their own arguments for at least as long as Maureen could remember. Her mother was apparently an unstable person who had deserted her husband and her children and now maintained no contact with them. In addition, her father had frequently been ill, and on at least one occasion in the past had been violent towards Maureen. It seemed probable that when Maureen was good she was ignored, and this for any child is unbearable. If she made enough noise and caused enough trouble she would get attention from one of her parents; true, the attention took the form of a shout or a slap, but this was better than being ignored as it meant that her existence was being acknowledged. By the time Maureen went to school she had been learning for five years that the way to make grown-ups take notice of you was to be naughty.

Maureen was a girl of average intelligence but there was never any chance of her gaining praise and recognition for good work. She soon found that when she was naughty at school she could make the other children laugh. Admittedly, they often got angry with her as well but Maureen had never had the chance to discover acceptable ways of getting attention. Her school was in a difficult area with a high turnover of teachers, so that she seldom had the same teacher for more than a term or two at a time. The succession of teachers tolerated Maureen and tried to find ways of interesting her, but when their patience was exhausted, they soon learned that a slap would calm her down, if only for a day or two. When Maureen did behave, her teachers tended to heave a sigh of relief, and wonder how long it would be before she had another set-to. In this way the school reinforced Maureen's experiences at home and she became more and more convinced that the way she could get attention was to be a nuisance, since being good was either too difficult, or was simply unsuccessful. Maureen's comprehensive school teachers recognised this as speculation but it did seem to be consistent with the known facts about her background. At a staff meeting the teachers agreed on two implications for Maureen's management at the school:

(a) Maureen's behaviour reflected her previous experiences and was largely designed to attract attention. If she did not succeed in getting attention in this way, this behaviour pattern would cease to serve any useful purpose for her.

(b) She would therefore need to find other ways of attracting attention to herself.

Now, ignoring Maureen's attention-seeking behaviour would only be successful if she could be given other and more legitimate ways to attract attention. Discussion at a staff meeting revealed that Maureen's English and maths teachers had very little problem with her. It seemed that in the most formal academic subjects she conformed willingly and could produce work of quite a good standard. The major problems occurred in practical subjects such as cookery, domestic science and so on. Teachers of subjects she liked said that she responded well to attention; for example she often asked to do jobs and had recently been a highly efficient register monitor for her class teacher. In the other subjects she was so often a nuisance that none of the teachers had thought of asking her to do anything special; at the staff meeting the teachers who found Maureen a particular nuisance agreed to find her some small but useful job to do, such as helping them to clear up at the end of the lesson, or, in art, putting out the paints at the beginning of the lesson.

It is tempting to give children extra attention or extra responsibilities only when they have done good work, yet are the children who derive satisfaction from doing good work the ones who most need their teacher's extra time and attention? Mr Franks had argued that the small extra jobs were too often given to the children who need them least. Maureen was not a clumsy girl, but she felt safer in the more academic subjects. Insecure children do sometimes feel threatened by practical subjects such as art which require more self-expression than the traditional academic subjects. Maureen particularly needed encouragement from teachers in practical subjects; when they started to ignore her attention-seeking behaviour, and at the same time started to give her attention, by offering a variety of small jobs, her behaviour showed a notable improvement.

Questions

1 Do you agree with the year tutor's assessment of Maureen's behaviour? Would caning her have "gratified and hence encouraged" her efforts to get attention? Even if the year tutor was correct, was he justified in refusing to treat Maureen in the same way as other girls, especially if others were being punished for less disruptive acts?

2 Would you feel differently about this if the school had abolished caning, and some other punishment (e.g. detention after school) was being suggested?

3 Should it have been necessary for the year tutor to ring up the junior school to ask for further information about Maureen? Could there be a danger in the junior school passing on too much information?

4 What reports should the junior school have received from the Social Services Department? What action should they have taken when they noticed bruising on her body?

5 How can a school foster links with hostile or apathetic parents? How might it have been possible to enlist the cooperation of Maureen's father at the start of her secondary school career?

6 Was the education welfare officer justified in refusing to visit the home on the grounds that Maureen's attendance had been perfect? Do you agree with the head's policy that teachers should not make home visits?

7 What is a supervision order? Why was it surprising that the divorce court did not make one for Maureen and her sister? Who would have carried out the supervision, and what would have been his legal obligations with respect to Maureen and to the court?

8 Was the social worker justified in refusing to reopen the case unless the school had definite evidence of cruelty or neglect?

9 Is it reasonable to believe that a shout or a slap is better than being ignored?

Do you think that children do "learn" to be naughty in this way? Would Maureen really have been ignored if she had not been naughty at home?

10 Do you accept that Maureen's primary school teachers reinforced the "maladjusted" behaviour which she had been learning at home? How might they have avoided this?

11 What other explanations are there for Maureen's behaviour? Do you think it is as rational as the case history suggests?

12 If Maureen had not been temperamentally "a lively, outgoing girl", would she have reacted against her family's problems in the same way? How might she have reacted if she had been a naturally quiet, withdrawing child? How important are temperamental differences between children?

13 Do you think the principles of reinforcement were being applied appropriately in the management solution proposed at the staff meeting? Would it be possible to ignore Maureen's attention-seeking behaviour?

14 Which of the two parts of the solution proposed at the staff meeting do you regard as most important?

15 If you were one of the teachers who found Maureen difficult, how would you feel about giving her small but enjoyable tasks to do, when other more hardworking children had requested them? How might your attitude have affected Maureen's behaviour? How might you alter your own attitude?

16 Would you call Maureen a "maladjusted" child? Is her behaviour the behaviour of a normal child?

James

Main points

1 A personality clash between a child and his teacher is not unusual. Pretending that it does not exist is not helpful.

2 Suggesting that a child changes class should not be regarded as evidence of his teacher's failure.

Mrs Hardy wondered if she was getting too old for teaching. She had been a part-timer for ten years, but now that her youngest daughter was going to a comprehensive school had returned to full-time teaching. Although she had someone to come in and "do" the house twice a week she was finding it a strain teaching all day and preparing her lessons after cooking a meal and listening to her four teenage children in the evening. She had an uneasy feeling, though, that her real strain was not the long hours but James and his gang.

James Wilkin was a noisy exuberant six-year-old, already one of the strongest children in the infant school. He was also highly intelligent, and Mrs Hardy was uncomfortably aware that she was not extending him in the classroom; he did whatever she asked with passable efficiency but seldom spent more time or effort than was necessary. The school ran an integrated day, but James always seemed to have done everything before. When Mrs Hardy did start him on something that would really extend him he took an immediate interest, but she found herself spending all her time on James with the result that there was soon a group of other children clamouring for her attention. When left to his own devices James was not always openly disruptive; he attracted other children away from what they were doing, and set up his own little group in a corner of the classroom. One of his friends had recently had his appendix out and James had visited him in hospital. James and three other children had played doctors and nurses for most of one morning, which was all right until James played the part of the ambulance rushing to hospital. Even this, though, was better than "Indians hunting buffaloes, miss", which had followed the story she had read the class about the American prairies. The trouble with James, Mrs Hardy reflected bitterly, was that as well as being big, extroverted, noisy and intelligent, he was also a born leader.

The other teachers were divided in their opinion of James. The majority view was that he was "all boy", a stereotype of all the attributes with which (as a feminist member of the staffroom explained) male-dominated society says boys should be endowed. Her colleagues were not fooled, though; although she dismissed James as a male chauvinist pig in the making (he regarded the girls as "sissy" and only allowed them to join in his games if it suited his immediate purpose), it was clear that Mrs Haslam secretly had a soft spot for him. On the other hand, other teachers were less tolerant. One of the reception class teachers thought he had a "nasty streak" in him. "He thinks of no one but himself," she said, "I've seen him knocking the little ones flying as he charges across the playground, and I've caught him threatening to bash them if they don't join in his game." The reception class teachers were known for their somewhat protective attitude, but they were not alone in their views about James. "Big-headed, he needs bringing down a peg", was another comment.

Mrs Hardy knew that James's mother also found him a handful. A few months previously she had asked for an appointment to discuss James's progress. The head and Mrs Hardy had seen her together and it had quickly become apparent that what she really wanted to know was whether James was as difficult at school as he was at home. A quiet, anxious person, she had sat on the edge of her chair throughout the interview, visibly embarrassed by the trouble she felt she was causing. The head had done her best to reassure her, saying that James did good work at school, even if he was a bit slapdash at times; as for the rest – well, "He's just all boy; you've got to sit on him sometimes!" "But he does such dreadful things," Mrs Wilkin had replied helplessly. She went on to explain that James had scribbled all over the sitting room wall after she had refused to let him play out after tea. "I know I was wrong," she said, "but I smacked him really hard. But it didn't do any good; he just said he'd run away from home!" Mrs Hardy knew just how James's mother felt, but didn't feel able to say anything, as this would imply disagreement with the head, who was busy reassuring her again that James was "just all boy".

One thing that did emerge from the interview was that James's father was a businessman who frequently had to spend prolonged periods away from home in London and on the Continent. He too was a retiring man, at least as far as his family life was concerned, and found James a handful. In contrast, James had a twenty-one-year-old uncle whom he idolised. Uncle Pete lived a mile or two away and visited regularly – in fact if more than three or four days went by without a visit James pestered his parents to ring up and find out why. Uncle Pete played rough games with James and took him on long walks and weekend camping expeditions in the Yorkshire Dales. A few weeks earlier he had walked twenty miles on Saturday and another fifteen on Sunday, and Mrs Hardy remembered well that he had been even more full of himself than usual on Monday morning.

Mrs Hardy knew that James was getting the better of her, and also knew that Mrs Haslam, who taught the parallel form, would be a better teacher for him. She knew that Mrs Haslam would not object to having James, but at the same time was sure the head would not view a transfer favourably. She could imagine the brusque reply: "You're as bad as his mother; all he needs is firmness. If I let it happen with this one, how can I refuse anyone else, or any parent, who asks for a change of class?" The logic might be questionable, Mrs Hardy reflected, but the head's reaction was not. Moreover, the head would be right if she accused her of being too like James's mother. Like Mrs Wilkin, she was everything that James was not: quiet, sensitive, interested in art and craft activities rather than PE and games. She was in fact more skilled at teaching the slow child than the extroverted high achiever like James, and although none of the teachers thought of him as a sensitive child, James had been quick to sense his teacher's preferences; in consequence he was even noisier with her than he was at other times.

Questions

1 What staffroom tensions often focus on part-timers? How can they be avoided?

2 What staffroom tensions often focus on married women when they return to full-time teaching. How can these be avoided?

4 Is the integrated day suited to a boy like James? Might he have been better off in a more formal class?

4 Have you ever found it a problem to "extend" an intelligent child? How could you advise Mrs Hardy?

5 How could the head discourage the over-protective attitude of the reception class teachers?

6 Do "big-headed" children need "bringing down a peg"? Are there better solutions to the problems they pose?

7 Would James's mother have been reassured by her interview with the head teacher and Mrs Hardy?

8 In Mrs Hardy's place, would you have wanted to attend the interview between the head and James's mother?

9 Mrs Hardy didn't want to be disloyal to the head; does it really matter if two teachers disagree in front of a parent or a class of children?

10 How might Mrs Hardy and Mrs Haslam be able to get round the head's likely objection to James changing class?

11 Do you think any children might do better with Mrs Hardy than with Mrs Haslam?

12 Does the problem lie mainly with James or with Mrs Hardy? Would it have been a bad reflection on Mrs Hardy to suggest a change of class for James?

13 Can you think of other children who have benefited from a change of class (or school) in the middle of the academic year? What preliminary discussions are needed to increase the chances of success?

Anthony and Simon

Main points

1 Withdrawn children can be helped at school even if they continue to live in difficult or unhappy circumstances at home.

2 A teacher's efforts to comfort and to sympathise with a withdrawn child may sometimes have the effect of making him even more withdrawn. The reason for a child becoming withdrawn in the first place may not be the same as the reason for him remaining in the withdrawn state.

3 A child's withdrawn state draws his teacher's attention to his need for special help; yet his tearfulness may be a much needed coping strategy as well as an expression of unhappiness.

After three months with a class of first-year junior school children Mrs Green felt that she was getting on well with all the children except Anthony and Simon. These two, however, had her completely baffled; whenever she asked them to do anything they would dissolve into tears; all her attempts to bring them out of their shell and increase their self-confidence seemed to have the opposite effect. They sat on their own in different parts of the classroom, would not play with other children, scarcely ever spoke, and generally seemed to live in their own unhappy world. Both boys were said by their infant school to be backward, but Mrs Green thought they were both showing only a fraction of their real ability. For example, she had once seen Anthony putting a jigsaw together when he thought no one was looking; he had worked quickly and logically, but when she walked up to him he immediately lost interest and said it was too difficult. Similarly, some of Simon's pencil drawings were skilfully executed and unusually detailed for a child of his age. He preferred never to use paints, but if pressed would only use dull colours such as brown or black. He disliked his teacher or the other children looking at his work, and frequently tore it up before anyone could see it; once when Mrs Green had put a drawing on the wall he had burst into tears, and she had felt obliged to take it down again to pacify him. Mrs Green felt that Anthony was the more sensitive, but also the more determined child, while Simon seemed more nervous and highly strung. Neither could read or write at all, perhaps because they never even spoke to their teacher.

Anthony

The school records showed that Anthony's father was a Major in the Army, while Simon's was a farm labourer. Mrs Green mentioned her anxiety about the two boys to the head teacher, and the parents were invited to school to discuss their progress. Anthony's father turned out to be a brusque man with a bristling moustache. He refused an invitation to sit down, and instead perched on a table so that he was on a higher level than Mrs Green. "What's all the fuss about?" he wanted to know. He quickly made it clear that the reason for Anthony's failure to learn to read was "all these modern methods". He told Mrs Green that it was disgusting for boys to do needlework and cookery, and said he simply couldn't understand how any children made progress when they were allowed to do what they wanted all the time! He described his own education in a succession of formal army schools, and explained that hard work and discipline had got him where he was; this was what Anthony needed too! He added, significantly, that he had entered the Army as a private, and claimed that without his formal education he would not have had the discipline to rise from the ranks. At this stage Mrs Green felt like going to look for Anthony to congratulate him on being so normal! Instead though, she said to his father; "I can see that you are a very determined man; do you think that Anthony is a determined child as well?" The reply was unexpected; Anthony it seemed often showed what his father described as "dumb insolence" at home; he would sit down, often crying, and refuse to talk to anyone; this would last for hours and nobody could get him out of it.

What light did this interview shed on Anthony's behaviour? His father seemed a cold, authoritarian person with little understanding of, or sympathy with the needs of a seven-year-old boy. The withdrawn behaviour which Mrs Green saw as a sign of unhappiness was seen by his father as insolence. Nevertheless, she thought, the father was perhaps more accurate than he realised; Anthony's tears and refusal to communicate with adults or other children might be his way of escaping excessive demands, and of showing that he was still a child. Yet it could also be a valuable weapon, because it defeated his father; the latter's universal panacea for all ills, "a little bit of discipline never hurt anybody", somehow seemed inappropriate for a child who was always miserable and tearful; the fact that his father recognised intuitively the element of determination behind the unhappy façade made it all the more baffling for him.

At home Anthony had discovered without realising it that he could escape difficult demands by behaving in this way. He had also discovered that he could use it to baffle and exasperate his father. As the rest of the family took their lead from father, this was a useful technique. (In a very similar way, much younger children refuse to perform when their parents are excessively worried about their toilet training.)

Mrs Green now realised that Anthony was behaving at school in the same way that he was behaving at home. The more withdrawn he became at school the more attention she was giving him, and the less academic progress he made. Anthony never seemed to get praise at home, and it was safer not to make any attempt rather than to risk failure and criticism. The more Mrs Green encouraged him to try things, the more determined he would become not to attempt them. When he next started crying she said, "You can come and see me afterwards if there's anything the matter, but otherwise you must join in with the rest." She then sent two other children to work with Anthony, and took no further notice of his crying or refusal to speak to her. On the other hand, she did make a point of praising him at least two or three times each lesson. To start with this was for almost insignificant things such as picking up a pencil, or simply opening his book when the others started to read. Gradually Anthony discovered that he was getting praise and recognition for small things he had achieved, but that crying and being miserable no longer secured him a lot of Mrs Green's time and attention. In the course of the next few months he discovered that she would be sympathetic if he went to her after a lesson, but that during the lesson she expected him to be getting on with other things. Gradually, as his self-confidence increased he became able to channel his aggressive feelings along socially acceptable lines; whereas previously he had never joined in playground games he now became one of the livelier, more boisterous members of his class. By June, like many withdrawn children, Anthony was not so much coming out of his shell as leaping out of it, and Mrs Green was beginning to wonder whether she could encourage him to calm down a bit.

Simon

It was Simon's mother who came to the school; she was a tense, nervous woman who told Mrs Green that she had been divorced for two years. Simon had seemed disturbed at the time of the divorce, and had blamed his mother for it; at the same time he had become withdrawn and un-communicative at home and his mother frequently found him in tears. He still saw his father every week, enjoyed the visits, but could not get on with his new stepfather who, for his part, felt hurt by Simon's rejection.

Like Mrs Green, Simon's mother and his stepfather had spent a lot of time trying to draw him out and make him more cheerful. They both worried a lot when he was ill, and his attendance record showed that this happened pretty frequently, usually due to minor illnesses like a cold or sore throat. Mother did say that there had been one time when he really came out of his shell; her own mother had been visiting for a month, and had "just let him get on with it". With her Simon had seemed a happy, lively child and his mother had been hurt and bewildered when he withdrew back into his shell soon after her own mother had returned to London.

Mrs Green realised that at the time of his parents' divorce Simon had needed extra affection and sympathy. But, as often happens, his mother had been too preoccupied to give it. Nevertheless, she was conscientious and when her little boy became ill she looked after him with loving care. When he seemed depressed or withdrawn she always did her utmost to reassure him and make him happier. Just as a hyponchondriac man becomes more hypochondriacal when he knows his wife worries about all his illnesses, so Simon found that the way to get the attention he needed was to remain in the withdrawn state; in this way he could be sure of his mother's (and his teachers') attention. How then could Mrs Green help him?

As with Anthony, the reply was paradoxical; instead of spending a lot of time trying to draw Simon out of his shell she now started to encourage him whenever he did something of his own accord or joined in a group activity. To start with she had to encourage him for very small things, which she would have taken for granted in other children; by degrees though, she found that he was doing more and more things for himself, and was ceasing to be an isolated member of the class.

Questions

1 Anthony and Simon sat in different parts of the classroom; would you have put them together?

2 Can you think of any other children who have been regarded as dull when they may really have been withdrawn or uncommunicative?

3 Why do you think Anthony lost interest in the jigsaw when his teacher walked over to him? Why might Simon have been upset about his drawing being put up on the wall? Was Mrs Green right to take it down?

4 Both parents were interviewed by the class teacher; should it have been the head? How much contact should class teachers have with parents?

5 Why might it be "significant" that Anthony's father had entered the army as a private?

6 How would you reply to a parent like Anthony's father who attacked the progressive ideals of your classroom?

7 What should a parent do if his child starts to cry for hours on end, and is unable or unwilling to give a reason?

8 Do you agree with the suggestion that Anthony "had discovered without realising it that he could escape difficult demands by behaving in this way"? Can you think of other examples in which a child has adopted a "disturbed" behaviour pattern as a way of influencing his interaction with adults and other children?

9 Is it fair to praise one child for something that might attract criticism if done by another? Could this have happened with Mrs Green's efforts to help Anthony?

10 How would you explain Mrs Green's interaction with Anthony in terms of reinforcement principles?

11 Why might Anthony have become one of the "livelier, more boisterous members of his class"?

12 Is it a contradiction to think of a child as withdrawn and aggressive at the same time?

13 The school apparently did not know about Simon's parents' divorce until two years after it occurred. How can schools be sure to find out about this sort of family problem at the time? What support might they have given

Simon at the time? Could they have arranged any help for his mother?

14 How else might Simon's mother have given him the attention and reassurance which he needed?

15 Can you think of other children who receive reinforcement for behaving in a withdrawn way from teachers or parents?

Janet

Main points

1 Major changes in a child's behaviour or attitude can go unrecognised if they are gradual.

2 Some depressed adolescents need specialist medical help.

3 The "house tutor" cannot take over responsibility for pastoral care. In the first instance responsibility must always rest with the class teacher.

Comments written in Janet's exercise books: "A poor effort; what's the matter?" "You have done better work than this!" "The exam is only three months away; you really must sort out your notes!" "Good quality, poor quantity!" "Untidy." Oral comments: "What on earth's been the matter with you lately? For goodness sake *wake up!*" "How many more times must I tell you that the French for 'a lot' is 'beaucoup', not 'beacop'?" "You entered for six 'O' levels, and the way you're going you'll be lucky to get any!" "You stay in this class just as long as you do your homework regularly; if you don't do it, you're *out!*" Well-intended sympathy turning into exasperation and anger: "If something's the matter, try telling someone about it; would you like to see Mr Peterson [the counsellor]?" "Would you like a teacher or the welfare officer to come and talk to your parents at home?" "Is it boy-friend trouble? Are you feeling all right?" "All right, don't answer, but just pull yourself together!"

Questions, criticism, anger, sympathy, exasperation: none had impinged more than faintly on Janet's consciousness in the last few weeks. She was aware of them all, and found them vaguely unpleasant and irritating; at the same time, she felt guilty at causing so much trouble, and thought that people must care about her if they could get so worked up. But as for doing anything about it, well, it was all too much. She probably would fail their rotten exams, but they were not important, as it no longer mattered what happened to her.

Ironically, Janet's teachers were close to understanding how she felt. Indeed it was their feeling that they couldn't "get through to her" that frustrated them so much. She was an able girl, but not exceptional; she was in the A stream of a formal academically orientated former grammar

63

school, now a neighbourhood comprehensive. (Her class was actually called 5g, but no one was fooled, least of all the children in 5a.) She had usually been around the middle in class order, and the same applied in her maths and French groups. She had been entered for six "O" levels, and no one expected her to have any difficulty in getting good grades. She was a quiet girl, often overlooked in a busy class, but attractive and not unpopular either with the boys or with the other girls. Hugh Webb, her house tutor thought she would stay on to take "A" level in English literature, history and geography, and then perhaps find a place in a college of education.

The deterioration in Janet's work was not sudden. She was a steady, reliable worker, but like everyone she had her ups and downs. Imperceptibly, the downs became more frequent than the ups. Sometimes the quality of her work was good but there was too little of it; at other times it was the other way round; she started doing only half her homework, or skipping it altogether; her English teacher realised with a slight shock that she had been sitting at the back of the class for the last fortnight, instead of the middle; she gave up her boy-friend – not a serious affair, but one that had been going on for several months; she often had to be told twice to do something – ridiculous for a promising girl in the top "O" level class! Because the deterioration was slow it went unrecognised, and it was only when an art teacher returned to the school after a prolonged illness that the rest of her teachers really started to ask if anything was wrong.

"Whatever's been happening to Janet Hubbard?" she asked. "She's lost all her energy and she looks glazed and ill. She used to do beautiful paintings, with lots of movement and colour, but all she could manage today was a lifeless copy of a picture in a magazine." When it was put to them like this, all Janet's teachers recognised that she had indeed changed over the last few weeks. What was worse, none of them had any idea why. Janet was the younger of two children (the elder had left school two years before), so they couldn't get any clues from a brother or sister. Her former boy-friend said: "She's all moody and boring; you get fed up with her," when someone asked him about Janet. Worry about home or exams were suggested as a possible reason, but no one had heard of any problems at home, nor had anyone expected her to have much difficulty with the exams. Neither her medical nor educational records gave any clues.

Hoping for help from Janet's parents, Hugh Wells wrote to her parents, inviting them to visit the school as he had been worried about her progress in the last few weeks. The next day Mr Hubbard telephoned to make an appointment. They fixed it for the following Monday. On Monday morning he rang up in great anxiety to say that Janet had been taken to hospital by ambulance at 11 o'clock the night before having swallowed over sixty aspirins. They had given her a stomach pump and she was all right, but they were keeping her in for another day for observation, and she was to see a psychiatrist on Tuesday morning. He and his wife had been worried about Janet for some time; she had lost her appetite and they didn't think she was sleeping well either, but they had never dreamt that it would lead to anything like this.

Hugh Wells was bewildered and upset, blaming himself for not having seen the warning signs earlier. "But for goodness sake, how many other moody kids have we got?" said one of the colleagues. "If we referred them all to the psychiatrist he'd soon think *we* were nuts! Anyway, you only took her for two lessons a week, didn't you?" The last point was true, and highlighted one of the flaws in the pastoral care system. The first point was less valid; the other moody children had always been that way; Janet had not, and the change should have been noticed earlier.

That Friday the school medical officer received a copy of the psychiatrist's letter to Janet's family doctor. The letter was brief but informative. He had examined Janet in his out-patient clinic and found her to be depressed. He thought it possible that the depression might be reactive to the death of both her grandmothers the previous autumn, exacerbated by anxiety about exams in the near future. However, in view of the presence of what he called "classical symptoms" of weight loss and interrupted sleep patterns over the last two to three months he could not be sure about this. He was prescribing an antidepressant and would see Janet again in two weeks' time. Meanwhile he advised a return to school at the beginning of next week, but as far as possible she should be allowed to work at her own pace.

Hugh Wells had a quiet word with some of the pupils in Janet's class, telling them not to ask her where she had been when she returned on Monday. He also telephoned her parents, and was told by her mother that the psychiatrist said it would be at least ten days before they could expect to see any change. However, she had liked talking to him, and seemed a little happier; she now felt she had someone she could turn to. Hugh asked how she felt about coming back to school and was relieved to hear that she had decided herself that this would be a good thing. Her mother agreed with his suggestion that it would be helpful if she and her husband came to the school on Monday to have a more detailed discussion about Janet's problems, in order to ensure better communication between the home and the school.

After making this telephone call, Hugh Wells went to the head and suggested a meeting of all the senior staff to discuss the implications of Janet's case for changes in the school's pastoral care system.

Questions

1 Do you think critical comments written in a child's (or adolescent's) exercise books have any effect? Are there any practical alternatives?

2 Can you think of other pupils who have gradually become unapproachable? How did you try to get through to them?

3 Is streaming desirable in a comprehensive school? What are the beneficial and harmful effects?

4 How would you label the classes in a comprehensive school? Do you agree with the way classes were labelled at Janet's school?

5 How could the school reorganise its pastoral care system to ensure that problems were recognised before they became acute?

6 What is needed in an effective pastoral system besides good communication within the school? Was it present in Janet's case?

7 The house tutor (or head of year) cannot know each child in his house individually; what should be his role *vis-à-vis* the other teachers in the school's pastoral care organisation?

8 How would you try to reassure someone who was having "exam nerves"?

9 Who could Hugh Wells have asked for specialist help when his colleagues noticed the deterioration in Janet? How can a school refer to an educational psychologist? Can a school refer a child to a psychiatrist?

10 Should Hugh Wells have told the other members of Janet's class where she had been?

Lillian

Main points

1 Children behave in different ways towards different teachers. The reverse is also true. An interaction process occurs between children and their teachers which affects the behaviour of both.

2 Bullying is a problem which cannot be overlooked. An easy and superficially logical reaction is to punish the bully; however, a closer look at the interaction between the victim, the bully and their teachers may reveal that the simple solution overlooks the real problem.

The way some of the third-year boys were bullying Lillian Drummond was getting out of hand, thought Mrs Wedge, the deputy head with responsibility for girls' welfare in a new comprehensive school. She really was a pathetic little thing, but today for the third time this week she had come to Mrs Wedge in tears, and only last month her parents had rung up to say that she was frightened of coming to school because of the way some of the boys teased her. Mrs Wedge felt that she couldn't altogether blame the boys, but this sort of thing couldn't go on. Earlier in the week her male counterpart had caned three of the boys concerned, "presumably", remarked one of the junior teachers dryly, "because he thinks that that is going to make them like her better!" Certainly the boys themselves had complained bitterly about Lillian: "She's always messing, Sir, you just get started with something, and she goes and interrupts." Just as certainly, Lillian was still complaining about being bullied, and one of the same trio had admitted thumping her just after Mrs Wedge herself had been taking the class for history.

Mrs Wedge was a strong, experienced but sympathetic teacher. Not even the most fractious of the fifth-year boys upset her. Earlier that term she had intervened in a fight between the school's two most difficult sixteen-year-olds; one of them had turned on her, and called her an interfering bitch. "Spell it!" she snapped, and both boys had dissolved into laughter and gone off happily together. But bullying was one thing that made her see red. It aroused her fiercest maternal instincts, and in the last week Lillian Drummond's plight had been making her seeth with righteous indignation.

That lunchtime Mrs Wedge went to the third-year tutor, and told him that something would have to be done about the boys in Lillian's class. Being a diplomatic sort of man he agreed with her and suggested that the first step would be to call a meeting of all Lillian's teachers so as to work out a common policy. There were in fact eight teachers who taught Lillian for more than one period a week. Three of them were probationers, two more had had less than five years' teaching experience , and the other three were senior members of staff, with posts of special responsibility. The PE teacher said that she had never really noticed Lillian; she did what she was told and seemed to enjoy PE, even though she wasn't particularly competent. The other children seemed to accept her willingly enough, and she had not noticed any bullying or victimisation. The French teacher, who had joined the staff from college in Lillian's first term had a similar impression. On the other hand, the three probationers were all agreed that she was almost the most disruptive and difficult girl in her year. "She's always shouting out, walking round the room, poking or pushing other kids, and generally making life hell," said one. The others agreed that the rest of the class derived vicarious pleasure from Lillian's exploits; they could always get her to do the things they were too frightened to do themselves.

At this stage Mrs Wedge started to wonder whether everyone was talking about the same child; certainly the Lillian who was such a behaviour problem to the probationary teachers was a far cry from the pathetic, bullied, victimised little thing that she knew. When her two senior colleagues both agreed with her that Lillian was the archetypal scapegoat, the natural victim, Mrs Wedge didn't know whether to feel relieved, or even more puzzled. "If it had been up to me," said one of the younger teachers, "I'd have caned Lillian Drummond and given the boys who thumped her some house points!" The deputy head with responsibility for boys' welfare said: "What I can't understand is why the boys seem to hate her so much; she certainly does irritate them in a number of underhand ways, particularly if they are interested in something, but as she is no real trouble in the classroom with me perhaps I just haven't noticed how much she does annoy them."

For the following fortnight the three senior teachers made a special point of watching Lillian in the classroom. She was always polite to them, and always did work of a reasonable standard, but she continually said and did things which irritated the other children. For instance, one day she "accidentally" took the exercise book of the biggest boy in the class, and started writing in it; when he complained she claimed that she had thought it was her book. Later the same day Mrs Wedge just managed to overhear her calling a boy at the back of the classroom a "fat faced twit", and in the afternoon break Lillian had gone to her complaining that the boy was threatening to "get her".

Lillian's teachers were puzzled by the paradox. In some some lessons she was a serious behaviour problem, and in others she seemed a poor, victimised, bullied little girl. Perhaps there is less of a contradiction in Lillian's behaviour if we ask what it achieved from her point of view. Adopting the role of class clown would give her a degree of recognition, even approval, from the other children. She would certainly have recognised their vicarious enjoyment in her exploits, and even though her popularity was shortlived, this was a lot better than nothing. With the more experienced teachers Lillian found herself unable to behave in this way – their classroom control was so good she simply could not get away with it. Nevertheless, she had discovered, perhaps without realising it consciously, that they got terribly upset and worked up about bullying. With the younger teachers she could call attention to herself by being a nuisance, but with the older ones she had to obtain recognition through being victimised. Thinking about it later, Mrs Wedge realised that Lillian's mother was rather over-protective, and would probably listen with sympathy to complaints from Lillian that she was being bullied at school.

Questions

1 What do you think about the teacher's comment on the punishment of the boys who had been bullying Lillian?

2 How might Lillian have felt when the boys were punished? Does punishment (particularly corporal punishment) for bullying create further anxiety for the victim? Is it effective?

3 What is your reaction to Mrs Wedge going to Lillian's year tutor, and to his suggestion for a meeting with all her teachers? What does this suggest about the school's disciplinary structure and its pastoral care organisation?

4 Should anyone else have been invited to the meeting?

5 What does the staff meeting suggest about communication within the school? How could it be improved?

6 Should anything else have been discussed at the staff meeting?

7 Lillian was being bullied, but her teachers had found clear evidence that hse provoked it; what should the school do about this? If it is right to punish one child for bullying, could it also be right to punish his victim for provocation?

8 What other explanations might there be for Lillian's different behaviour with different teachers?

9 The case history implies that the more successful disciplinarians prevented Lillian drawing attention to herself by disruptive behaviour, with the result that she made herself into a scapegoat in their lessons. Is this too simple a view? Can you think of similar instances in which children have behaved in different ways with different teachers?

10 What positive qualities has Lillian got? How might the school build on these?

11 What reasons might there be for Lillian behaving in a disruptive way, and attracting aggression from other children?

12 Accepting that the school needs to know more about Lillian's behaviour at home, what aspects of school organisation could have contributed towards her problems?

13 How far does children's behaviour reflect the attitudes of the staff towards them, and towards each other?

14 Can you think of any teacher who attracts resentment from his colleagues similar to the resentment which Lillian attracted from other children?

Michael

Main points

1 Some children suffer when they put too much effort into their school work.

2 Highly competitive children often opt out of things at which they know they cannot excel.

3 Self-centred children are sometimes helped by an opportunity to help other children.

"Michael Leach's trouble is that he was born fifty years too late, and into the wrong social class; he'd have loved a really oldfashioned competitive prep school with marks for everything, from singing and games to tidyness and maths. His parents would have loved it too. He's lost here – no uniform, no class order, no marks even when he does a good piece of work. He wants to compete all the time, and we won't let him; no wonder he's aggressive!" The speaker was known both for her instant judgment on any topic under the sun that she happened to overhear in the staffroom, and also for the tenacity with which she stuck to her original judgment. Her advice was given most readily about children she had never had to teach. It did not matter that Kevin Jordan, Michael's teacher, was more experienced and had less difficulty with troublesome children.

The idea had in fact already crossed Kevin Jordan's mind, but he had dismissed it as too simple. Michael was an individualist, and individualists were never loved by teachers at formal, oldfashioned schools; in that sort of place Michael's rebellion would have become open and unmanageable; at Tom Holden Junior School he could at least be contained, and his progress was undeniable. In many ways he was a star pupil; his creative writing and maths were both outstanding, and he had picked up German from a set of "Teach Yourself German" records which his parents had bought before their last holiday on the continent. He was also highly competitive, never satisfied unless his work was not only better than anyone else's, but also seen to be better than anyone else's. Allied to this was the verbal aggression which he constantly used to tease and provoke weaker children. He was a master at the barbed, cutting phrase which would make someone else feel silly and inferior. Occasionally another child lost his temper and hit out at Michael but the challenge was seldom accepted; Michael would retreat in tears to the nearest teacher who usually ended up reading his assailant a lecture on not losing his temper, even if he had been called an unpleasant name. He seemed to have a knack of creating a competitive situation out of nothing, and his attitude was copied by some of the other more talented children who wanted to know: "Why should he get away with it, sir?" and strove to outshine him. Paradoxically, he opted out of most of the formal competitions that did take place in the school. The reason was not difficult to find; with few exceptions, such as chess which he won with no difficulty, they involved team games. Not only was Michael rather a clumsy ten-year-old, but the cooperation with other children which they required was beyond him.

Michael never did things by halves. His good work was done with great care and conscientiousness; on the other hand, subjects which did not interest him were done in a hasty, slapdash manner which would have placed him in the bottom 25 per cent of the class, if any such order had existed. Predictably, the things he took little care over were the things in which he had little natural aptitude. When he had difficulty with something that interested him, or when another boy excelled him, he often became so angry and frustrated that he was on the verge of bursting into tears.

Kevin Jordan knew from Mrs Leach as well as from his school medical record that he had suffered from asthma and miscellaneous allergies until he was nine or ten. The allergies had been to pollen, and various grasses and trees; they had foiled his one known attempt to join an out-of-school activity with other children. This had been three years earlier when he joined the school cubs, but had spent a week sneezing and wheezing after his first full day in the country. However, following treatment at the local hospital this problem had largely cleared up though he still had to take antihistamines.

Both Michael's parents had visited the school frequently. They ran a hardware shop not far away, and had once explained that they had both left school at fifteen, but were nevertheless determined to make a go of the business. The shop was, in fact, modestly successful, but both parents worked fulltime in the day, and the evenings were often occupied with orders, accounts, and VAT. Michael and his brother went to their grandmother after school; she was getting old, though, and did little apart from give them tea. By the time they returned home at half past five, Michael was irritated and on edge, eager to pour out everything that had happened at school: "Gran's so slow, and she doesn't seem to understand what I tell her!" he had once complained. His stories about school would not have surprised his teachers; he complained of bullying, the lack of interest from Mr Jordan when he did something good, and too much boring art, craft and PE. Mrs Leach alternated between sympathy and frustration, at one moment wanting to go up to the school and demand that the bullies be controlled, and at another wanting to slap Michael for his ceaseless and exhausting nagging and complaining. This inconsistency had also been apparent in school; she had told the head she was worried about how Michael would get on in the comprehensive school if he stayed so aggressive and so easily frustrated; yet she did not want to follow her neighbour's advice and request an appointment with a psychologist "in case all the fuss and attention makes him worse". The head did not feel inclined to persuade her, since he thought other children had greater need of the psychologist's time.

"Do you think Michael's a problem we've just got to live with, or is there something we can do for him?" Kevin Jordan was talking to the head during the lunch hour after an incident which Michael had provoked by crying in frustration at the end of maths lesson when a particularly complicated problem had defeated him. With his customary perceptiveness, Michael had countered a teasing remark with a comment on the other boy's squint; touched on the raw, the other boy had hurled a book at Michael's face, cutting his mouth. "If it's really true that none of the other kids like him, and he really is an isolate," remarked the head, "then I suppose the only way he can cope with life is by dominating other children – and if he can't achieve that by doing good work, he'll do it with his tongue. He won't join in any of the out of school activities, and he hates games, so it's hard to see how we can help him to get on better with other kids." After some further discussion Kevin Jordan suggested tackling this by getting Michael to help a younger child with something. "If he's got to dominate, we might as well help him do it constructively," he said. The idea of Michael Leach helping another child willingly, let alone a smaller one was an intriguing one. In the end, though, they decided that he might be more willing to help a younger child (provided it was not his brother) than one of his own age.

When Michael next did a particularly good piece of creative writing, Kevin Jordan asked him if he would like to help Miss Rawson, the remedial teacher, in the library in the first half of the afternoon when his class was normally doing art or craft work. Michael agreed enthusiastically. Miss Rawson was expecting him; she kept him busy writing words and questions in some of her children's books, and helping others find the books they wanted from the shelves. At the end of the session she asked him if he wanted to come every week, but warned that she would make him earn his living. A month later she reported that Michael was a willing, helpful, patient assistant. Unfortunately, though, there had been little change in his behaviour outside Miss Rawson's group.

Questions

1 Is there any teacher at your school who specialises in instant judgments? Are his judgments usually right?

2 Do you know children who have suffered because you (or one of your colleagues) formed an opinion about

them too hastily? How should a school guard against this?

3 Do you know any children who *wanted* a more competitive, traditional system? Would these children have been *helped* by such a system?

4 Do you agree with Kevin Jordan's assessment that Michael would not have settled in a formal, oldfashioned school? Do you agree with his reasons?

5 Michael was an individualist. Does the fact that many great men were unhappy and unsuccessful at school have any implications for schools' attitudes to individialists?

6 Do you think individualists are attracted into teaching?

7 What is the most common reaction to a child who is "skilled at the barbed, cutting phrase which would make someone else feel silly and inferior"? Is it the most constructive reaction?

8 When Michael provoked another boy into hitting him, his assailant usually ended up in trouble, and this must have been reinforcing for Michael. How would you tackle that problem?

9 Is there ever a case for class orders?

10 How would you describe the interaction between Michael, other children, and the teachers in terms of reinforcement principles?

11 How might Michael's medical history have contributed to his present problems?

12 If Mrs Leach asked you what she should do about Michael's complaints, how would you advise her?

13 Mrs Leach was inconsistent towards Michael; can you see similar inconsistencies in your own interaction with any children?

14 Do you agree with the solution proposed for Michael?

15 Why do you think Michael's helpfulness did not generalise beyond Miss Rawson's group? What would you do next?

Dennis

Main points

1 Every story has two sides, but the child's side is not always heard.

2 Corporal punishment can create more problems than it solves.

Sir Ken Griffith Comprehensive School,
Mornton,
Exshire

The Director of Education,
County Hall,
Exshire

Dear Sir,

Dennis Richmond (1.1.61)
111, High Street, Mornton

I am writing to report the indefinite suspension from this school of the above pupil. Yesterday afternoon he swore at Miss Rhodes, an experienced member of my staff, and subsequently refused to accept punishment from his Year Tutor. On being told that his parents would be sent for he accepted punishment, but two minutes later made a violent and unprovoked attack on Miss Rhodes, who had merely told him to leave the corridor and go to his classroom. In the course of this assault her glasses were broken, and she received a severe bruise on the nose, for which she received medical attention.

This is the third time that this boy has attacked members of my staff, and I submit that it is neither fair nor reasonable to expect staff or pupils to put up with his unreasonable brand of behaviour. You will see from the attached reports that he is antisocial and a menace in other ways as well. He has sworn publicly on numerous occasions; he bullies girls and younger boys, and is determined to cause the maximum amount of friction within the school wherever he has an opportunity.

I suggest that he should be transferred to some other type of school, which is better equipped to cope with his sort of behaviour. I shall be pleased if you will give this matter your immediate attention.

Yours faithfully,

D. Tamworth,

Headmaster

Mr Tamworth enclosed an impressive list of Dennis's misdemeanours with his letter to the Director of Education. The reaction in the office was one of awe; Mr Tamworth had expelled boys (and girls) before and was known for his hard-line views on trouble-makers, but they had never received a letter like this. Unfortunately, there was very little they could do. Dennis was already fifteen, and at this age no special school would consider him. The Divisional Education Officer knew that the head teachers' bush telegraph would already have been working, and he could therefore not hope to persuade another school to give Dennis a trial; in any case, with this sort of record he did not think a trial at another school could be justified. All he could do was arrange for Dennis to be placed on home tuition; this meant that a teacher would visit him at home for two hours twice a week. "But that's just giving in to him," exploded Mr Tamworth disgustedly when he heard.

Among most of Dennis's teachers, the reaction was one of profound relief. "The only thing is that it should have happened two years ago" was one comment. Nevertheless, the staffroom was not united on the issue. The notes of dissent were muted; after all, the head, his deputy, the year tutor and the senior heads of departments had all been determined for many months that Dennis Richmond was "a bad 'un" and if you were a teacher who wanted to get anywhere you didn't offend all these people by expressing what they would certainly regard as woolly, "progressive", and left-wing views.

One of the teachers who thought Dennis might have had a raw deal was Henry Sawford. Now only two years away from retirement, he had come to Sir Ken Griffith School after a bad illness five years before. He had previously been the deputy head of a large secondary modern school, and had welcomed a chance to return to classroom teaching for his final few years in the profession. For the last two years Dennis Richmond had been a competent and conscientious member of his maths class. At the end of the first year he had recommended that Dennis had the ability to move into a CSE, or possibly even GCE maths group. The suggestion was not accepted: "You're not getting rid of him on to me I'm afraid!" he had been told by the head of the maths department. Henry Sawford had sensed, rather than felt, that Sheila Vernon also sympathised with Dennis. She had been teaching for two years and this was her first post. She contributed little to the staffroom but had proved herself successful with some difficult classes. She had taught Dennis English for three terms, and although he had called her a "cow" in her first week with the class, this little storm had been weathered without external assistance and they had developed a good understanding; if she didn't nag him, and didn't ask him questions in front of the class, he would give her good written work whenever she set the class a piece of free writing. However, she was never to read his work aloud to the class.

A week after Dennis's expulsion, some teachers were talking about him in the staffroom, and overhearing them Henry Sawford asked Sheila Vernon if she remembered the three incidents when he had attacked members of staff. She looked at him, clearly on her guard. "Why do you ask?" she replied cautiously. "Well, I never had any trouble with him myself, and I just wonder if he didn't have a raw deal here." Sheila Vernon walked over to a corner of the room so that they wouldn't be overheard. "The first time," she said acidly, "was when the fat dinner lady with a mole called him a naughty little boy in front of the first-year girls and tried to make him stand on a chair. He told her the truth about herself, so Collins [the Year Tutor] tried to cane him and David put a chair over his head! The second time was when that supply history teacher got a cheap laugh at the expense of his friend by saying that all West Indians were descended from slaves. Dennis told him to 'piss off out of this school', so he went to get the head, who caned him in front of the class. As the head turned to go out, Dennis overturned the table and went for the supply teacher. I gather he made quite an impression. The third time was last week. I was teaching next door to Miss Rhodes's social studies lesson. You know how thin those partitions are. I could hear every word, and she was nagging and challenging him from the start of the lesson right up to the end when he shouted: 'Perhaps I'll get some fucking peace now!' as he went out. Collins caned him with Miss Rhodes as a witness, but after he'd finished she had to open her mouth again, only this time she found she'd put her foot in it!"

"In other words," said Henry Sawford, "every attack followed corporal punishment. You'd have thought the message might have got through after the first incident, that this wasn't the answer for Dennis. It looks as if we've got slow learners in our midst, doesn't it?"

Sheila Vernon asked what he thought would happen to Dennis now he was on home tuition. "He'll become a focal point for all the truants and apprentice criminals in the district," replied Henry Sawford in a quiet, resigned way, "and he'll get into trouble with the police, and when he goes to court they'll make a supervision order, which will mean that he has to go and see a probation officer once a week. He'll still be left on his own all day, though, so he'll get into trouble again, and then he'll probably be put into care and sent to an approved school. I suppose I should call them community homes, now."

A month later they heard on the school grapevine that Dennis was on supervision for theft from gas and electricity meters. Seven months later they heard that he had been before the juvenile court again, this time for breaking and entering shops and warehouses; the court had made a care order, and he was awaiting placement in a community home some eighty miles away.

Questions

1 Does Mr Tamworth's letter tell you anything about Mr Tamworth?

2 What investigations should a local education authority carry out on receiving a letter like this?

3 What sort of a school do you think Mr Tamworth had in mind when he recommended that Dennis be transferred?

4 Has the school any legal or moral responsibility for a child after excluding him? Has the local education authority any responsibility?

5 Mr Tamworth was disgusted when Dennis was placed on home tuition. Should this have come as a surprise to him?

6 Is the open expression of opinion in the staffroom often as restricted as it appears to be at Sir Ken Griffith School? How would you expect this attitude to affect teaching style? How might it affect the pupils?

7 Sheila Vernon reached an understanding with Dennis; did she go too far in trying to accommodate him?

8 Would it be reasonable to expect the other teachers to try to reach a similar understanding with Dennis?

9 Dennis was not accepted for a CSE or GCE maths group. What does this imply about the expectation of the senior teachers? How could this have affected Dennis? What action could a year tutor have taken when he recognised that serious trouble was likely?

10 Do you agree with Henry Sawford that Dennis had a raw deal at the school?

11 If you were Dennis's parents, what would you have done on hearing about each of his three assaults on teachers?

12 Do you think the school would have treated Dennis in the same way if his parents had been articulate and influential? Can you think of other instances where a parent's reputation (good or bad) has influenced the way a child is handled?

13 What sanctions could have been used instead of corporal punishment?

14 Should women teachers be allowed to inflict, or witness, corporal punishment on adolescent boys?

15 Why does Henry Sawford say he should call approved schools "community homes" now?

Charlie

Main points

1 A minor injustice can have effects which escalate in unpredictable ways.

2 Some children achieve success by deliberately provoking teachers into punishing them.

"I've never known a kid talk about his parents like that; he said his mother was a lazy bitch and his father's mouth was bigger than the Mersey tunnel. All I'd said was that he seemed a bit fed up today, and he just flared up at me. When I asked what was wrong he said: 'Ask bloody Evans', and stormed out of the room."

Jill Peters, a maths teacher in her second year was talking about an incident which had occurred at the end of her previous lesson. Charlie Knight was a thorn in the flesh of many of the staff, but before they could expand on his many vices, "bloody Evans" came into the room to warn his colleagues that they might have trouble from Charlie. Two days earlier Charlie had been given half an hour's detention at the end of school for skipping a PE lesson. The teacher, Martin Davison, had readily admitted being over-hasty; he was struggling with a heavy cold, his car had broken down on the way to work, and he had been having a bad time with two fifth-year classes before taking Charlie's second-year group. He had seen Charlie at the start of the lesson and told him brusquely to hurry up and get changed; and mumbling something which he didn't catch, the boy had gone in the direction of the changing room. In fact, Charlie had been mumbling that his father had given him a note asking the school to excuse him PE as he had hurt his foot. The library, which was the correct place for him to be in the circumstances, lay in the same direction as the changing room. At the end of the lesson Martin Davison had returned in disgust to find Charlie sitting in the library listlessly looking at a book. "Knight, half an hour's detention and now get out of my sight before I make it something worse," he had snapped.

Charlie had done his detention without complaint; his complaints had been reserved for his parents on his return home. Mr Knight, a bulldozer driver, did not have happy memories of his own school days and listened sympathetically. He was on edge, tired after a sleepless night with his own father who lived opposite and was slowly dying of cancer. It had been a long, painful illness, and the old man's mistrust of pain killers added considerably to the burden of nursing him. The unfairness Charlie had suffered at school provided a convenient focus for his father's anger and frustration: "I'll go up and sort that bloody crowd out!" he had promised. Charlie went to bed content.

But Mr Knight in his own home was a different man from Mr Knight in the setting of his own childhood and teenage failure. In Mr Evans's study he became hesitant, apologetic, eager to see the school's point of view and escape. Mr Evans had listened politely and promised to look into the complaint. He had then taken the chance to acquaint Charlie's father of the school's serious concern about his wayward son. Attached to each child's record card the school kept a list of important, and not so important, incidents in each child's school career. Charlie's list was a long one, consisting almost entirely of misdemeanours. Seeing this list, Mr Knight had rounded indignantly on his son, confident of himself now that he was no longer attacking authority, made him apologise for the trouble he had caused, and told him to "just wait" until he got home that evening. Mr Evans had tried to stem the flow, explaining that his intention was to see how Charlie could be helped, not to haul him over the coals for old offences. Unfortunately he had to take assembly and did not have time to pacify Mr Knight, whose parting shot was that Charlie needed more of the sort of punishment that schools used to give when he was a boy. Charlie had left the room with fury and contempt written all over his face.

The staff had a good deal of sympathy for Charlie, even though their sympathy was not altogether untinged with a painful sort of amusement. Martin Davison had been feeling bad about his treatment of Charlie before Mr Knight's visit and now felt even worse. Against the advice of two senior colleagues, who thought he should just forget it, he decided to apologise to Charlie at the start of the next lesson; the punishment had been in public, and so the apology should not be in private.

To his relief, the class accepted the apology in silence, except for one unsympathetic comment that "he had it coming to him anyway, sir". At the end of the lesson Charlie volunteered to help put the apparatus away. He repeated this offer on subsequent occasions, and became one of a small group who regularly helped the PE teacher for the last twenty minutes of the lunch hour on two days a week. Having initially been an uncharacteristically quiet member of this group, Charlie gradually opened out. One day, the boys were talking about school as they helped with the equipment, and the teacher overheard one of them refer to "your friend Evans, Charlie". Charlie had stiffened, hesitated, and then said bitterly: "He told me to behave myself because my parents were worried about my grandpa; that's got nothing to do with him." The incident passed off without further comment, but the intensity in Charlie's voice had not gone unnoticed. A fortnight later the conversation turned to punishment, and Charlie had stoutly defended the right of teachers to cane. He had objected, though, to them hitting boys in the classroom for minor offences – a practice which was not as rare as the head would have liked to believe – and again the PE teacher noted the same intensity in his voice.

Charlie had indeed been caned on a number of occasions, but he had also attracted as much informal corporal punishment as the rest of his class put together. Talking to his colleagues, Martin Davison found consistent reports; Charlie occasionally did something really serious (like throwing a brick through a window), but his real talent was for the minor irritations that make teaching a strain instead of a pleasure. "He never seems to know how far to go," said Jill Peters; "I've hit him twice; each time he looked as if he could kill me, and he shut up for the rest of the lesson, but he managed to give the impression all the same that he thought he'd won! What's more, *I* went away feeling he had, too!" Thinking of the incident which had led to him taking an interest in Charlie, Martin Davison felt that he'd been here before; had Charlie deliberately provoked him into giving an unfair punishment so that he could then say the school was in the wrong? This suspicion was strengthened by the French teacher, who had punished Charlie after he had misused a piece of audio equipment; it was only later that he discovered that the boy had not been present when the class had been given instructions, but he too had noticed the look of aggressive satisfaction in his face when he had been punished. Not only was Charlie full of complaints about the school, Martin Davison realised with growing bewilderment; with disconcerting frequency these complaints seemed to have some justification.

Questions

1 How do you think a subject teacher should react when a child expresses such intense resentment against his parents? Should this be a matter for the pastoral care staff?

2 When have you acted unfairly as a result of pressures which were nothing to do with school?

3 If Charlie *had* skipped the PE lesson, would the punishment have been appropriate?

4 What were Charlie's motives in doing his detention without complaint?

5 Have you come across other parents who become tongue-tied on entering the head's study? How do some teachers unintentionally place barriers between themselves and parents? Is the anxiety only on the part of the parent?

6 Have you ever apologised to a class for some unfairness? Should you have?

7 What are the areas of anxiety which might have prompted Martin Davison's two senior colleagues to advise him to forget about his incident with Charlie?

8 Do you think Charlie was justifiably bitter at Mr Evans telling him to behave himself because his parents were worried about his grandpa?

9 School was a temporary focus for Mr Knight's anger, but was not the real reason for it. Is there any parallel in Charlie's behaviour?

10 Should a head teacher tolerate

"informal" corporal punishment? How can he stop it?

11 Why do you think Charlie provoked teachers into punishing him? Why might he have looked satisfied?

12 Do you know any other children who have successfully provoked a teacher into giving an "unfair" punishment?

13 Are further investigations needed into possible reasons for Charlie's behaviour?

Mark

Main points

1 Violence is not always a sign of gross maladjustment. It is sometimes a normal reaction to intolerable circumstances.

2 When a child is under continuous stress his school is potentially the most important source of support.

3 School and social workers need to set up recognised procedures for keeping each other in touch about developments that affect children.

Mark's family was known to every social work agency in the town; each of them had tried to effect some change, and each in turn had failed. The NSPCC file went back sixteen years to the time when the eldest child was just three months old, and before that a child care officer from the old Children's Department had been seeing Mrs White, who had spent most of her life in care before becoming pregnant at the age of seventeen and marrying two months before the birth of her first daughter. Since then social workers had been in and out "like yo-yos", as the head of Mark's comprehensive school remarked bluntly. Currently Mr White was on probation for theft, and a social worker from the Social Services Department also had a responsibility for the family. The NSPCC and Family Service Units had bowed out, and the diocesan moral welfare lady had not been back after her first visit. The local Child Guidance Clinic had said that the children were at least as normal as could be expected, and probably a good deal more normal than it was reasonable to expect! Apart from Mark, now nearly fifteen, and his sixteen-year-old sister there were three other children. All had been poor attenders, and it was rare for all the children to be in school at any one time. Three years previously Mr White had been taken to court over his children's non-attendance, and although he was able to pay the £2 fine out of his social security payments without difficulty, since then none of the children had been so irregular as to justify any further action.

In a poor area the children were exceptional for their poor clothes and unkempt appearance; they frequently had head lice, and had all had impetigo and scabies on several occasions. At Mark's junior school the other children had refused to sit near him because he smelt, and the head had arranged for him to have a bath at the clinic attached to the school; when Mrs White heard about this she had come storming in, complaining that both Mark and she were being victimised, and threatening to call the police if the school ever made similar allegations about her not keeping her children clean. Mr White worked from time to time, but had never held one job for more than a few months. The latter part of his own education had been in an approved school. Mrs White had been to an ESN school and had been violently resentful when the Education Department had transferred two of Mark's younger brothers to one. The head of the ESN school thought that both children were making good progress, and that if they came from a less deprived home would be able to cope in a normal school. Mark himself was known to be of above average intelligence.

Nevertheless, as the educational welfare officer had remarked to the head eighteen months previously, the pattern of Mr and Mrs White's own childhood was not being faithfully reproduced in the lives of their children; against all the odds none of them had yet been received into care nor had any of them gone to residential schools. Indeed it was one of the paradoxes of the family that despite all the dirt and squalor there was a degree of family unity which would have been welcome in many materially better homes. This unity was at no time stronger than at moments of acute stress, when Mrs White became severely depressed and had violent outbursts. She had three times been admitted to hospital following a drug overdose, and on one occasion had spent a month in the city's psychiatric hospital. She had discharged herself, and since then out-patient appointments had seldom been kept.

Mark's educational progress had been erratic; there had been times, sometimes several months on end, when he had made good progress in the classroom, and had played an active part in a number of out-of-school activities. At these times he was well liked by other boys, and recently he had started going out with a girl in another class, who was planning to stay on to take "A" levels. "Could be the making of him," remarked one of his teachers. There were other times though – and these also lasted several months on end – when Mark was tense, moody, uncooperative both in and out of the classroom, and apparently quite genuinely unable to take part in, or even understand, the day-to-day work of his class. At these times many of his teachers came to think that he must really be rather dull. He had been involved in occasional fights both at his junior school and at the comprehensive, but his aggression had never been regarded as anything out of the ordinary.

Halfway through his fourth year Mark became involved in a fight that was out of the ordinary. What had started as a minor argument with his girl-friend escalated when he suddenly shouted at her to "get the hell out" and hit her in the face, breaking one of her front teeth. The boys who separated them said Mark had been like a wild animal. Mark refused to explain what had caused his outburst: "She gets on my nerves whittling on like that." The head sent for Mark's parents, and his father telephoned the next day to say that he could come up on the following Tuesday, in five days' time. As Mr White didn't usually accept invitations to come to the school the head accepted the delay. Meanwhile Mark had two further outbursts. The first was when an older and bigger boy had told his younger brother to "get washed you dirty sod"; Mark had come off worst in the ensuing fracas, but it had taken three staff and two fifth-formers to hold him back. The other incident was on the Monday, towards the end of a maths lesson when the teacher noticed that Mark had not done anything and said: "Isn't it about time you made a start, Mark?" Mark had jumped to his feet shouting abuse, hurled his chair at the teacher's head, and stormed out of the school. Following this incident the head wrote to his parents, sending a copy of the letter to the chief education officer and the chairman of his governors, excluding Mark from school for a fortnight.

Hearing about Mark's suspension the social worker made another visit to the family. What she knew, but the school did not, was that Mark's sister had been taken to court on a shoplifting charge three weeks earlier, and the court had made an interim care order, which meant that she was taken into care for three weeks while the authorities obtained reports. It was likely that a care order would be made when she returned to court, and placement in a community home outside the city was probable. What the social worker did not yet know was that this had precipitated another of Mrs White's recurrent bouts of depression, and she had been incapable of taking any interest in family life. The social worker did not know Mark well; most of her time had been spent with the parents and the oldest daughter. Mrs White and her daughter had always been dependent on each other, and as the oldest child in the family, Wendy had played an unusually, perhaps unnaturally, large part in bringing up her younger brothers and sisters.

On her visit to the home the social worker discovered that Mark had had a fight with his mother the previous evening, following his mother's attempt to take yet another overdose; Mark had struggled with her, removed the pills from her mouth, and eventually thrown them down the toilet. Throughout this his mother had been hysterical, and was still in an acutely distressed state. The younger children were even less cared for than usual, and Mr White was, allegedly, at work. It was clear that Mark, as the oldest in the family now that his sister was away, had been bearing the brunt of the family's pressures, and had been doing his best to keep the family together. Faced with unbearable tension and responsibility at home, sensing that his family was disintegrating around him, any additional stress in the form of criticism or teasing at school was more than he could stand. It was as though the safety valve had blown off. The mild stress

84

which under normal circumstances he would have managed with no difficulty, now became the straw which broke the camel's back. Following his exclusion he had not returned home, and slept rough in a derelict building. He had only reappeared shortly before his social worker's visit.

The social worker was tempted to take Mark into care there and then, but for a variety of reasons she decided not to do this. What she did do was telephone the Family Service Unit and ask them if they could give the family intensive help for the next four to five weeks. Also, she visited the school to explain to the teachers what had been happening in the household over the last three to four weeks. She expected, and got, a mixed reception from Mark's teachers; on the one hand they were sympathetic to his difficulties, but on the other hand they felt that this sort of violent behaviour would have a bad effect on the other children and adolescents in the school. One of the younger teachers, in his probationary year, expressed sympathy for Mark and said that he had always been helpful and conscientious in his lessons. Earlier Mark himself had told the social worker that he particularly liked Mr Cooper. The social worker asked if Mr Cooper could be enabled to take a special interest in Mark. The head was dubious; this sort of pastoral care with a disturbed adolescent called for a high degree of maturity and skill and he felt that it should be a more experienced teacher. Eventually, and against the better judgment of some of his colleagues he agreed to give it a try. Mr Cooper would be free to see Mark during the assembly on Tuesdays and Fridays; in addition whenever Mark felt himself building up for an explosion he would be allowed to leave whatever he was doing and go to Mr Cooper's class. Mr Cooper would give him something to do, and Mark would have to get on with this until the midmorning or afternoon break, or the lunch hour; Mr Cooper would then find time to talk to him, and try to release the tension without another outburst occurring. This, the head and social worker thought, should help them keep in closer touch about crises in the family while at the same time giving Mark some much needed sympathy and support.

Questions

1 The local Child Guidance Clinic said the children in Mark's family were at least as normal as could be expected. Would you describe his behaviour as "maladjusted"?

2 What are the parents' legal obligations with respect to school attendance?

3 Which branch of the Education Department has a responsibility for school attendance?

4 What action would you take if a child in your class came to school in exceptionally poor clothes?

5 If your school did not have a bath what would you do about a child who was being ostracised because he smelt?

6 What should the primary school head have done when Mrs White complained about Mark being victimised? Should he have insisted on Mark continuing to have a bath?

7 Mrs White was resentful when two of her children were transferred to ESN schools. What other problems might they have had to face when they went to the special school?

8 Do you know other children whose social and educational performance was as erratic as Mark's? Are the reasons comparable?

9 How can a teacher guard against dismissing a child as dull when his poor progress is attributable to problems at home?

10 After Mark's attack on his girl-friend what immediate action could the head have taken which might have prevented the subsequent outbursts (apart from suspending him)?

11 Mark's sister had left school; should the social worker have told the school about the interim care order?

12 Could the social worker have done anything to obtain temporary medical help for Mrs White? Would it have helped if she had been forcibly taken into a psychiatric hospital? Would it have helped to take Mark into care?

13 Do you agree with the explanation for Mark's outbursts?

14 The teacher selected to help Mark was in his first year of teaching. Do you agree that young and inexperienced teachers can do important work in a school's pastoral care system? Does a young teacher have any advantages which a more experienced person does not?

15 Have you any criticisms of the solution which is proposed to help Mark?

Billy

Main points

1 School has an influence on what children do out of school.

2 The help a teacher can give may be limited, but it is still worthwhile.

"Billy," said Dick Maddock, head of Flipton Church of England Junior School, with the air of one who has been through it all before, "is one of the crosses we have to bear." The young curate who had come to take assembly nodded sympathetically. Having spent half an hour in the Sutcliffe household the night before, he was not going to contradict Dick Maddock. "Mrs Sutcliffe told me last night that their Peter had just been sent down for thieving; what with Billy making his second appearance last week, and Peter yesterday she's getting to feel a bit persecuted," he remarked. "I'm afraid it'll take more than a few persecution feelings to get her and Mr Sutcliffe to change their child-rearing practices. We'd better go into assembly before I get depressed thinking about that family!"

Billy was the fifth of seven children. His two older brothers had been to community homes (formerly approved schools), and both his sisters had appeared before the juvenile court, though they had so far escaped with nothing more serious than twenty-one days remanded in custody on an interim care order. At the age of eleven, Billy was maintaining the family tradition. His first court appearance had not followed his first offence – that had been four years earlier, before he reached the legal age of criminal responsibility – but had been only a month after his tenth birthday. On this occasion the magistrates gave him a conditional discharge for stealing a toy pistol and some caps from Woolworths. "It means that if I get done again I get done for that too," he explained to Mr Maddock on his return from court. The second time Billy "got done" the charge was breaking and entering three houses and "doing" the gas meters. The court made a care order on the older boy he was with, and placed Billy on supervision for two years. "They let me off again!" he explained, "but I've got to go and see this social worker every week."

Mr Sutcliffe was a well-known but unsuccessful petty criminal with a history of several short prison sentences. When not in prison he occasionally took labouring jobs, but never held them for long and was more often living on social security. This must have been supplemented by other income, since the home was well furnished and both parents smoked over forty cigarettes a day and frequently went to the club in the evening. Mrs Sutcliffe was a worn, tired-looking woman, only too glad of the things that her husband brought into the home; she had long since learned not to question their origin, and she turned the same blind eye to her children's delinquencies. It was not that the Sutcliffes did not love or care about their children; they had simply inherited a life style in which this was the only possible way to live. Indeed, in its own curious way the family was happy and united, far happier than some of the wealthy, lonely alcoholics Dick Maddock had known in his previous post as deputy head of a school in the city's most affluent district.

In a sense, Billy would have been deviant had he not started stealing; at the very best he would have been an oddity amongst his family and their friends. (How many children are called "maladjusted", when they are merely conforming to their cultural norm!) When he first got into trouble with the police (three years before they could charge him), the Education Department had suggested that he might benefit from a residential school for maladjusted children. The offer was repeated after his first court appearance, but on both occasions the Sutcliffes turned it down indignantly: Billy was their son, and they were not going to send him away. If the court sent him away that was another matter altogether, but until then the family would stick together.

Dick Maddock was inclined to blame the social worker when the court failed to remove Billy from home at his second appearance: "I suppose they're trying to keep the family together," he grunted, "why can't they help the kid before it's too late?" His report for the court had made clear that Billy had stolen a dozen things for every one with which the police had charged him. "He regards all teachers and most children as fair game;" he wrote, "we have had complaints from three local shopkeepers, but they have refused to prefer charges." He was disillusioned, however, when the social worker visited the school and told him that she too had recommended a care order. "Four of my predecessors have worked with this family for the last ten years," she explained wearily, "so I don't know what they expect *me* to do now!" Like Dick Maddock, she was resigned to waiting for Billy to commit a more serious offence, which would force the court to make a care order.

Billy's class teacher, June Fawcet, was unimpressed by this counsel of defeat. "It's ridiculous to say he can't be helped," she exclaimed angrily. "Of course he'll do something worse if people take that attitude." Dick Maddock replied: "It looks as if you've got yourself a job, June! Tell me how this school can help Billy and I'll do my best to help you carry it out – but don't ask me to let him go on the school camp! I'm not taking that risk!" This was said as a parting shot. Billy had wanted to go on the school camp in the first week of the summer holidays and his parents were willing to pay for him. His behaviour within and out of school was so unpredictable, though, that Dick Maddock had put his foot down.

June Fawcet had no idea how to start helping Billy, but decided to concentrate on the biggest problem, namely his stealing. If he could get over this nothing else would seem important; he had a certain nuisance value, for shouting out, "accidentally" bumping into other children, losing his books and so on, but it was the endless accusations and searches whenever the police visited, or a teacher or child lost something, which really raised the staff's blood pressure.

June Fawcet knew that Billy liked her, though he often pretended not to. She also knew that he enjoyed several of the school's out-of-class activities, though he was often banned from attending them. In particular, he looked forward to the table-tennis club at lunchtime on Wednesday, the outing to the swimming baths on Thursday morning, and the Friday evening youth club. In addition, the youth club had a full day outing one Saturday a month. June took her class swimming herself, and helped run the youth club. The teacher responsible for the table-tennis club was a friend of hers. She decided to use Billy's enjoyment of these activities as a way of controlling his stealing. She put her plan to the head: "I'll give him two stars each day there are no reports of him stealing. Each time we hear that anyone, inside or outside the school has the slightest suspicion of him stealing he'll be 'fined' five stars. He will be able to 'buy' attendance at the Wednesday, Thursday and Friday activities for three stars each, and these stars will then be transferred to a separate 'deposit' chart. The fines cannot be paid out of these stars, but if he has earned a total of thirty-five, he will be able to 'buy' a place on the Saturday outing; those stars will then be placed in a second 'deposit account'," and, June Fawcet added with a glint in her eye, "eighty-five will enable him to come on the camping trip." Dick Maddock did some rapid arithmetic. Billy could get a maximum of ten tokens a week, and the end of term camping expedition was ten weeks away. He decided that he was quite safe. "If he gets eighty-five I'll recommend the education committee to pay for him to have a flight in Concorde!" he said cheerfully.

Billy obviously thought June Fawcet was a bit simple when she explained all this to him. "You mean, you're going to give me two stars for not knocking off, miss?" he asked. Being a realistic child he accepted this idea as an adult whim, and lost no tokens for two weeks. As each activity cost three stars, he was one star in credit at the end of each week. In the third week he was caught stealing a Mars Bar from a local shop on Monday; he was only two stars in credit on his current account, so his "fine" meant that he had to earn three tokens to pay off his debt, and another three before he could buy his way into any activity. He realised with a shock that he would have to miss table-tennis and swimming, and would only be able to go to the Friday youth club if he lost no more stars.

Billy lost no more stars for the rest of term. His general behaviour in the classroom and playground seemed to improve as well, and he caused no problems in the school camp. But the rest of the summer holiday was too much for him. A fortnight before the end of term he was arrested climbing out of the back window of an electrical shop with a £40 radio under his arm. When he appeared in court he asked for three further offences to be taken into consideration, and the magistrates made a care order without more ado.

Questions

1 What is an interim care order?

2 What is the age of criminal responsibility? What can be done if a child is out of control before this age?

3 Is Billy correct in his explanation of the meaning of a conditional discharge?

4 What is meant by Billy being on supervision for two years?

5 Do you believe it was really the case that "in its own curious way the family was happy and united"?

6 Do you think a residential school for maladjusted children would have helped Billy? What sort of school organisation might have been most suitable for him?

7 Both head teacher and social worker wanted Billy removed from home. Do you think this was to help Billy, or to protect society?

8 Billy was not to be allowed to go on the school camp; does it often happen that the children who most need these holidays are the ones who cannot go?

9 Was June Fawcet right to concentrate on the biggest problem first, or should she have started with one of the smaller problems?

10 What do you think of June Fawcet's programme for Billy? Do you think this sort of approach is ethical?

11 Who could June Fawcet have asked for advice when planning her programme for Billy?

12 What alternative approaches could have been tried to control Billy's delinquency?

13 Do you think it was all worthwhile?

George

Main points

1 Imaginative use of classroom activities can help children whose problems occur outside the classroom.

2 A child who cannot get on with other children needs "remedial education" just as much as a backward reader.

3 It is necessary to understand why a child is stealing in order to see how best he can be helped.

"George's trouble is that he's such a hopeless thief; I don't believe he has ever taken anything without getting caught!" Betty Oldham's voice contained exasperation as well as humour as she told the head of Lawson Junior School about George Wilkinson's latest exploit. Having stolen small change totalling 30p from Peter Bradshaw's pocket during the mid-morning play time, he had offered 10p to each of Peter's friends as they went home for lunch. The two boys were happy to accept the windfall, and spend it at the corner shop on their way back to school. When they returned Peter had discovered his loss and an inquiry was already in progress. Within a few minutes the finger of suspicion was again pointing at George, who soon confessed with the show of penitence his teachers knew so well.

George was small for his age, and other boys had found they could get him angry by calling him "titch". Betty Oldham tried to keep this to a minimum, but she could not control what happened out of the classroom. He was one of the duller boys in his class of nine-year-olds, and attended the remedial reading group on three mornings a week. His stealing had been a problem ever since he joined Lawson Junior School a year ago. At first only small things went missing, rubbers, elastic bands, pencils, paintbrushes, pieces of plasticine and so on. For two or three weeks his teacher was puzzled; when she saw two of her star pupils using a set of missing paints which a child in another class had lost the day before she was alarmed and bewildered. George was soon recognised as the culprit, but the odd thing was that he never kept any of his loot; he always gave it away, even though the grateful recipients of his bounty seldom had the slightest qualms in informing against him. Had Betty Oldham been strictly accurate, she could have said that George was a highly competent thief – he was very seldom caught in the act – but his distribution system needed an overhaul!

The teachers at Lawson Junior School had sympathy for George. The school was situated in a tough but stable area, and George was the only pupil in his year who had spent more than two or three weeks in "the homes", as children and staff referred to the Social Services Department's residential establishments. He was taken into care at the age of five when his mother had to enter a psychiatric hospital with schizophrenia. This had started when his father was given a two-year prison sentence for receiving stolen goods. Mrs Wilkinson spent over a year in hospital, and then discharged herself against the advice of the consultant psychiatrist. For the next few months she tottered between her own home and George's children's home, growing visibly weaker as each month passed. On his release from prison Mr Wilkinson found his home in a state of extreme squalor and his wife in a state of advanced mental and physical exhaustion; nevertheless he confounded the confident expectations of the prison authorities and the local authority's social workers by tidying and re-decorating the house on money saved first from his social security payments and later from his job with the council. He gradually nursed his wife back to health, and had George home for weekends. However, it was not until three years after his son's original reception into care that he was able to return home permanently.

Knowing George's background enabled his teachers to regard his persistent stealing more tolerantly than they might have done otherwise, but this did not help them see how to help him. They wondered if he was upset by continuing problems at home, but this did not seem to be the case. His parents were always ready to come to school, and the head's impression was confirmed by the social worker who said Mrs Wilkinson had now recovered completely from her illness, while Mr Wilkinson seemed to be a reformed character, holding a steady job as a driver in the council's welfare fleet. Material standards in the house were adequate, and both parents showed George demonstrable affection, which he appeared to return. They were as worried as his teachers about his continued stealing; every available punishment had been tried, including the slipper at school and "a belting" at home, but although he was always penitent there was no lasting evidence of improvement.

No one was in doubt as to why George took things. He was never known to keep any of his loot; instead he tried to "buy" the friendship of other children by offering it to them. In the short run this was successful since it brought him temporary popularity, but in the long term it had the effect of making other children mistrust and avoid him. The trouble was that the more other children mistrusted him, the more lonely and isolated he felt, and therefore the more he needed their acceptance; but the only way he had ever been able to gain any acceptance was through "buying" it with the things he took from other children.

"Can't we teach George how to make friends with other children, so that he won't have to buy friendship in this silly way?" Betty Oldham asked the head. The head put the question to a psychologist who was visiting the school to see another child. His reply was unexpected: "Mrs Oldham runs successful free drama sessions with her class, doesn't she? She can use this talent with George. I'd have thought she might be the ideal person to teach him the social skills which nine-year-old boys use in their everyday relationships with each other!" The head looked puzzled, but sent a child to ask Betty Oldham to come to his office. The idea of role play sessions to show George new ways of getting on with other children appealed to her: "I could get some children to act the wrong way to do something, and the others to do it the right way," she said, "and then the first group could try again. The kids will enjoy thinking of situations to act."

On the first occasion she tried this, one of the girls suggested: "How to make a new kid feel at home, miss." There was a noisy session in which seven children showed how they thought the "new kid", (selected by Betty Oldham for his cheerful resilience), could be made to feel thoroughly miserable in his new school. Subsequently a different group tried to make him feel welcome. "And now," said Mrs Oldham, "we'll do it again, but this time I want two volunteers, one to show a new kid who settles in quickly, and one to show a new kid who becomes lonely and gets unpopular."

The session was an undoubted success (largely as a result of her previous drama work with the class), and she was glad to see George taking more interest than usual when the class was concentrating on the successful and the unsuccessful new kids. At the end she said to him: "I think you felt sorry for that new kid who couldn't settle in." George nodded. "Do you want to come in at quarter past one with three or four other boys and practise the better way to do it?" George's face lit up: "Yes, miss!"

The psychologist had asked the head to let him know if George was still stealing in two months' time. The head thought this was merely postponing the day when something would have to be done about George, but was pleasantly surprised to find that his stealing had become less frequent. Whether it was due to Mrs Oldham's weekly drama sessions was a different matter, but he had to admit that George was starting to mix more easily with other children of his own age.

Questions

1 What rules should a head teacher make about children bringing money to school? How should they be enforced?

2 How far should a teacher go to protect a child from teasing? What should be done about the offenders?

3 Why did George get called "titch"? Would it have been fair to say: "It's all his own fault – he asks for it"?

4 What are the possible effects on a child when a parent is sent to prison? How can a teacher be aware of these? What help can the school give?

5 Would Mr Wilkinson have had the right to remove George from the children's home whenever he wanted to?

6 Do you know other children whose behaviour problems do not seem to be in any way related to stresses in the home?

7 "To understand all is to forgive all." Is it?

8 Should corporal punishment ever be used for stealing?

9 Do you agree with the assessment of George's reasons for stealing? Are there any other explanations?

10 Do you agree with the psychologist's suggestion, and with the way Betty Oldham used her drama sessions to help George?

11 What are the dangers in this approach?

12 Can you think of other children who might be helped by imaginative use of drama sessions? Is this something which only an exceptionally experienced teacher could do?

13 How might aggressive children be helped to learn more sociable behaviour through drama sessions?

Colin

Main points

1 Lack of suitable teaching at school increases the likelihood of truancy, even when the truancy starts as a reaction to problems at home.

2 Children can often cope with their parents being physically ill better than with mental illness.

Constable Henstock was indignant, but the note of admiration in his voice was quite unmistakable. "Proper little club he'd got going in there, carpet on the floor, four chairs, magazine pictures on the walls, bottles of pop and glasses, and to cap it all they were just fitting a new lock to the door to keep intruders out! It wasn't scruffy either; there was a pack of cards neatly on the table and somebody had made out a list of rules – no gambling for more than 20p a time, subscription of 5p each visit, and you'd to promise not to snitch!"

Unfortunately for Colin Saunders, one of his friends had snitched! The school had given up making detailed inquiries when Colin was not present, but when his friend Michael did not turn up for two days he was questioned closely on his return. Michael wasn't a strong character and quickly admitted that he had been with Colin, in Colin's club at the old Plaza Cinema. The Plaza had been empty for the last seven years; it would have been bought up by a property developer when it closed, but local councillors thought it might be of some historic interest and ever since there had been a legal and political wrangle over whether it should be demolished; meanwhile it had gradually become more and more dilapidated. The windows and doors were boarded up, but it appeared that Colin and his friends had found a way in.

Colin had helped the police with their inquiries for two hours after being discovered; the sergeant interviewing him wished that all children and adolescents were as helpful. Colin readily explained how he had got into the Plaza, forcing an old coalgrate, and then fixing one of the exit doors so that he could get in from the street without difficulty. The club was in the old projection room. "All the rest was too big or too dirty," he explained. He claimed to have bought the lock on the door with the subscription money, and when the policeman said he didn't believe him he had given the names of four other boys who could corroborate his story. The club had been open about a fortnight and in this time eight or nine boys had attended, but Colin was the only regular. The others were known to their schools as regular truants, and four of them were already known to the police. When the policeman asked him facetiously about the attendance register Colin explained apologetically that it was not up-to-date because the boy whose job it was to keep it hadn't been coming lately! However, Colin told the policeman where to find it, and the school exercise book was duly recovered.

Mr Smith, Colin's head teacher, was more concerned about the other boys than about Colin, who he had long since decided ought to be in a special school. All the same, he had to admit that this was inconsistent with his previous estimation of Colin. In school he was easily overlooked, indeed on the infrequent occasions when he did attend he was conspicuous only for his talent in fading quickly away into the background. He had never been a behaviour problem, and was polite to teachers, but no one felt they knew him well and his class teacher commented that even if he did come regularly he was the sort of boy no teachers would ever get to know well. The other children seemed to regard him in much the same way as the teachers, a pleasant enough person to have around, not someone to be afraid of when you're up to something, but at the same time not someone you'd ever get to know well. They occasionally taunted him, calling him "Wagger" and a welfare officer had heard another boy telling him that he'd "get done" when he next went back to school. This never seemed to worry Colin, who always remained remarkably self-sufficient.

Colin was a non-reader; when he left his primary school two years previously the head teacher had commented on the confidential record card: "Colin's attendance has been atrocious throughout his entire school career; he has never had a chance to make any academic progress, for the simple reason that he is never here to make it. We tried to motivate him by placing him in the group taken by the peripatetic remedial teacher and he attended for a few weeks, and even started to make progress. Then his mother went into hospital, and he started truanting again and we had to give the place to one of the other children. For his last year with us he has been in a group of slow learners, but has made virtually no progress. His reading age (Burt) is 4·8." In his two years at a secondary school Colin had been as consistent as ever; his reading age was now 5½ on Schonell's Test, and he had attended on twenty-three out of the last 125 possible occasions.

The educational welfare officer found Colin's case the most depressing he had come across. His father was a morose man who drank heavily and frequently came home drunk on Saturday nights. He was sometimes violent to his wife, though he had never been known to hit Colin; however, he took no interest in his son's education, saying it was up to his mother or the authority. He did nothing with his son in the evenings or during the school holidays, and had even forgotten his last birthday. Colin was an only child; an older brother had been killed at the age of six when Colin was four; he had slipped his mother's hand, run out into the road, and died under a bus. Another child, four years younger than Colin had died at the age of six weeks from a bronchial infection. Mr and Mrs Saunders seldom talked to each other, in fact the welfare officer thought they only lived together because they both lacked the energy to separate.

Mrs Saunders suffered from acute depression but refused to see her general practitioner about it; it was not unusual for her to spend days on end sitting silently in the corner of the living room weeping almost continuously, unable to do any cooking or housework. She was acutely anxious about Colin. "I've lost all the others," she said nervously to the education welfare officer, twisting her handkerchief into little knots as she spoke, "so what'll happen if they take Colin away?" Privately, the welfare officer thought that what would happen would be that she would commit suicide, and indeed this was one of the reasons that he had resisted suggestions from the school and his chief officer that the parents should be taken to court over Colin's non-attendance.

Colin's education had already been discussed at length. Six months before the latest incident Mr Smith had called in one of the authority's educational psychologists, in the hope that the psychologist would place Colin in a special school. The psychologist had been sympathetic but unhelpful. Colin, it seemed, was certainly not ESN (his IQ was 95), nor did he have any specific perceptual or physical difficulties that could explain his total lack of progress in reading. The psychologist had thought a boarding school place was desirable, but had not been willing to recommend a residential ESN school, and a school for normal children would not contemplate accepting a thirteen-year-old who could not read. In any case it was doubtful whether his mother would agree to him going away to school. Mr Smith had said that it was disgraceful that the junior school had not done more to help Colin, and that it was ridiculous to expect a secondary school to help so retarded a child, particularly when there were such severe social problems. He had no facilities to teach a child like Colin. Whatever the psychologist's reply lacked or did not lack in accuracy, it made up for in tactlessness. Over three-quarters of the authority's secondary schools were able to pay heads of remedial departments as much as the deputy of any primary school in the authority; further, the remedial teachers in secondary schools were on the whole better trained and more experienced than their opposite numbers in the primary schools. Mr Smith had as many scale posts on his staff as any of the other schools, and if he was sincere in his wish to help children like Colin he would establish a good remedial department in his school, even if this meant a slightly lower salary for one or two teachers in his newly established sixth form.

Two weeks after Colin had been found in the Plaza, Mr Smith and the educational welfare service heard that he was to be charged with breaking and entering. Following the usual practice, the court was asking the school and the welfare service for any information and advice they could give.

Questions

1 Most schools forbid pupils to bring cards on to the premises. Does this have the effect of making them more likely to gamble?

2 Have you come across any other "truants' clubs"? In the light of what is known about truancy why is it not surprising that Colin was the only regular attender at his club?

3 How can a class teacher make himself more sensitive to the needs of children who fade into the background?

4 What are the reasons why some children fade into the background? Does it always matter?

5 Do you think Colin really was "remarkably self sufficient"?

6 Colin's reading age on Burt's Graded Word Reading Test was 4·8 when he left his primary school; after two years in his secondary school it was $5\frac{1}{2}$ on Schonell's test. Why does this constitute no progress?

7 How would the circumstances of Colin's older brother's death have affected his mother?

8 What can we infer about the inter-actions between different members of the family? What is Colin's contribution?

9 Why do you think Colin started to truant?

10 Which of the potential sources of stress in Colin's home do you think would be the most difficult for him to cope with?

11 Do you think the psychologist was justified in refusing to recommend Colin for a place in a school for ESN children?

12 Was Mr Smith fair to blame the junior school for not having done more to help Colin? What else could they have done?

13 Do you agree with the psychologist that a secondary school should be able and willing to teach a boy like Colin? How many teachers should be doing remedial work in a secondary school of 1,000 pupils?

14 What advice do you expect Mr Smith and the education welfare officer to give the court? Do you think it would be the right advice?

Nigel

Main points

1 There is seldom a single cause for attendance problems.
2 Truancy (being absent from school without the parents' knowledge or consent), is a relatively uncommon cause of unjustified non-attendance.
3 Teachers and education welfare officers need to work together in cases of unjustified absence from school.

"Hey, Miss, can I have next week off to look after my baby brother?" Wondering vaguely why Alfred had to ask everything in a voice loud enough to be heard in the next classroom where the deputy head was taking another class of fourth-year juniors, Miss Robson asked, "Do you want to?" "Not likely!" replied Alfred emphatically, if illogically. Miss Robson thought that she ought to let the matter rest, but her curiosity got the better of her; after all, this was a craft lesson and since the visit of the craft advisers the month before the staff had felt freer to experiment in these sessions. "Why do you ask, then?" she said. "Well, Miss," said Alfred, eager to be in the limelight, "Nigel says he didn't come to school last week because he had to stay at home and look after his baby brother. I reckon he's nuts; I can't wait to get away from mine." Unexpectedly, Nigel butted in:, "You wouldn't say that if you'd had to stop him falling into the fire." Someone else said it was Nigel's mother's job to look after the baby and Miss Robson quickly changed the subject.

Nigel had always been a bad attender, but just lately, three months before transferring to the secondary school, things were getting a lot worse. Over the last three months he had averaged only two days a week in school, and had not been present at all for a fortnight before this conversation took place. Miss Robson had asked to see his medical record at the beginning of the year. Apart from being slightly shortsighted in one eye Nigel had nothing wrong with him physically. However, three years earlier his family doctor had referred him to a psychiatrist at his mother's request. A copy of the psychiatrist's report had been sent to the principal school medical officer and was attached to the file. Mrs Smith, it appeared, had taken Nigel to her doctor because she was unable to get him to go to school; each morning he shouted, cried, claimed to feel ill and eventually rushed to the toilet and was violently sick. After the initial scene, when it was clear that he could stay at home for the rest of the day he quickly recovered, played happily, and accompanied his mother on shopping expeditions. The psychiatrist had drawn attention to the disturbed family relationships. Nigel's parents had separated when he was two and divorced shortly afterwards. Nigel had gone to live with his father and another woman. They had married as soon as the divorce was finalised, but the marriage turned out to be a disaster and by the age of five Nigel was back with his mother. When the psychiatrist saw him at the age of nine, he had not seen his father or stepmother for nearly a year. The psychiatrist diagnosed "'school phobia', arising from a separation anxiety caused by worry about his mother's health". Mrs Smith, it appeared, had herself been showing signs of depression – tearfulness, losing weight, seldom eating – and the psychiatrist thought this was a reaction to the failure of a relationship which she had hoped would lead to a new marriage. The report also said that Nigel had been seen by a psychologist who had found him to be of above average intelligence, with a full scale IQ on the Wechsler Intelligence Scale for children over 120. The psychiatrist had prescribed drugs for Mrs Smith and arranged for a social worker to visit her regularly. He also saw Nigel a few times, and the boy's attendance improved. The case had been closed at the end of the year.

The education record showed that Nigel's attainment in all the basic subjects had been below average since he started school. Three years earlier there was a note in the head's writing stating: "Psychiatrist says school phobia, but always seems quite happy when he's in school. No sign here of above average IQ."

Miss Robson had met Nigel's mother on open nights, and knew that the family circumstances had changed since he had seen a psychiatrist. Eighteen months ago she had had another son, and was hoping to marry the father as soon as his divorce came through. This was expected to happen before Christmas, but meanwhile he was living with his parents and visiting Nigel, his mother and the baby most evenings and weekends. Miss Robson had wondered whether Nigel's attendance at school was deteriorating because his mother was depressed again, but the education welfare officer had visited the home and reported no signs of this. The head was reluctant to refer Nigel to the educational psychologist. "He's had his share of the cake already, and there are more urgent cases, who he might be able to do something for," he had replied when Miss Robson broached the subject.

Miss Robson wondered if Nigel really had to stay at home to look after the baby. Remembering that she had asked some of the class to write about "my baby brother" earlier in the term, she looked through Nigel's old English book and found the passage: "I like holdering Tommy when he crys. He makes faces at me and I like helping with barthing him. Once I had to stop him goering to near the fire when my mum had gone out."

Miss Robson wondered how many twelve-year-old boys enjoyed holding their baby brother or sister when they cried, let alone helping with the chore of bathing them. By coincidence all the fourth year were being shown the BBC Merry Go Round sex education films, and the last one was programmed for the following week. After it, Miss Robson asked the class, "How many of you have baby brothers or sisters?" About six children put their hands up, but not Nigel. "Nigel has, too, Miss," chimed in Alfred, helpful as ever, especially when there was a chance of stirring things up a bit. Miss Robson asked Peter, a confident, self-sufficient boy how he had felt when his sister was born. "Fed up!" replied Peter with a cheerful grin, "she was always yelling; but she's all right now Miss." Some of the others told the class how they had felt, and then Miss Robson asked Nigel. He shrugged his shoulders non-committally – "All right," he answered briefly. "I reckon he was jealous, miss, because his mum was busy with the baby and hadn't got so much time for him! Hey, what's that for?" Nigel had thrown an exercise book at Alfred's head and was now standing up, white with anger, more animated than Miss Robson had ever seen him. "You sod, I wasn't," he shouted. She made the two boys sit down and then explained to the class that it was natural to be jealous when a baby was born. Some people got upset when they felt jealous and tried to be very kind and helpful to make up for it. "I was like that for a bit," said Peter, "my gran said that sticks and stones could break her bones but thoughts could never hurt her, and I like her now anyway; we have fights at bedtime!" Nigel gradually calmed down and by the end of the lesson Miss Robson thought there was a look of relief on his face.

Over the next few weeks Nigel was away from school for only three days. The following week he was absent on the Monday and again on Tuesday, so the head asked the welfare officer to visit. At his fourth knock, Nigel opened the door. His mother was out, she had gone to the hospital to visit an aunt, Nigel explained, and he had to stay at home to look after the baby. Yesterday he had had to look after the baby while his mother went shopping. Mrs Smith confirmed Nigel's story when the welfare officer visited again in the evening. He decided on a firm line, and told her that she had a legal obligation to send Nigel to school. If she needed someone to look after the baby she must find someone else. If this happened again he would have to advise the Education Department to prosecute her.

For the rest of the term Nigel's attendance was almost perfect, but Miss Robson had an uneasy feeling that further problems might arise when he transferred to the secondary school next term.

Questions

1 What does the first paragraph tell you about staff relationships in the school? Do you think it tells you more about Miss Robson or about the head and deputy?

2 What access do most teachers have to a child's school medical records? Is this sufficient?

3 Do you know other children whose absence from school is due to genuine illness for which there is no apparent physical cause? What are the probable reasons?

4 What does the head's note on Nigel's record card suggest about communication between the school and the psychiatrist? How could it be improved? What else should have been done for Nigel at the time of his original refusal?

5 What are the likely reasons for Nigel's poor academic attainments?

6 If a child in your class wrote as Nigel did about his baby brother, would you consider it a reason for making further inquiries?

7 What do you think of the way Miss Robson handled the discussion after the last Merry Go Round film?

8 If a teacher was not confident about holding this sort of discussion, what else could she do?

9 Do you agree with the line the education welfare officer took with Mrs Smith?

10 Does a parent ever have the right not to send a child to school?

11 What is the legal obligation of the local education authority if a child is not receiving education?

12 What sanctions can be taken against parents who refuse to send their children to school? What sanctions can be taken against children or adolescents who refuse to attend school?

Kaye

Main points

1 Fear of a particular lesson is not always caused by fear of the teacher.
2 It is not always helpful to protect children from the truth.

3 Anxiety may persist even when the original reason for it has been removed.

"What have you been doing to Kaye Milburn?" the educational welfare officer's tone was both puzzled and accusing as he buttonholed two of Kaye's teachers in the staffroom. Both of them looked at him blankly. "If you asked what we'd do if we ever saw her I could give you an answer," replied Keith Tyson, the woodwork teacher, "but she hasn't turned up for the last five or six weeks." "Well she turns up for everyone else," countered the EWO. "Look at this register; the only times she's gone missing are when she has woodwork and PE. I found out from her mother yesterday evening that she always comes home at the right time. Her dad played hell with her, and she eventually told him she spent the time walking round the park when she's not in school."

The two teachers felt irritated. They both prided themselves on their good relationships with their pupils, but here was someone telling them – in front of their colleagues – that a child was so frightened of them that she was truanting during their lessons. "He's a terrible fierce man is Keith!" shouted someone from the end of the table.

"All right, let's talk about it away from this rabble," Keith said sourly. As they walked out Donald Chester, Kaye's year tutor, came up the stairs, and asked if the EWO had got anywhere the previous evening. "If you knew all about this why didn't you come and tell us?" This time the accusing question came from Hilda Bentley, Kaye's PE teacher. The excuse that they had only realised themselves at the fortnightly lunchtime welfare meeting, and neither had been in school in the afternoon, was accepted grudgingly. "The funny thing is," said the EWO, trying without much success to ease the situation, "that she doesn't seem to be frightened of either of you!" Donald Chester said he was planning to see Kaye during his free period later in the day. The case puzzled him, because neither

Keith Tyson nor Hilda Bentley usually upset a girl like Kaye. The bigger and lazier boys sometimes complained that Keith was too hard on them, but there had never been complaints from girls. Hilda was an experienced teacher who sometimes deliberately appeared to lose her temper when she thought this would shake an apathetic child or class into action, but she never did this with quiet and conscientious, if dull, children like Kaye. As both Donald Chester and the EWO had expected, neither her woodwork nor her PE teacher had any explanation for her truancy in their lessons. They both remembered her vaguely as a cooperative, retiring twelve-year-old who was sometimes called "limpy" by the other children, because she had been born talipes and still had a slightly clumsy way of walking. Her junior school had carried out group intelligence tests, and there was a note in her record card saying that her IQ on a non-verbal test was 85. Her academic attainments were commensurate with this. She was not seriously withdrawn, though she had a tendency to fade into the background, and was well liked within her own small circle of friends. Inquiries during the lunch hour revealed that none of Kaye's other teachers had any problems with her.

Later in the day Kaye was not forthcoming when Donald Chester saw her in the interview room – a bare, boxlike place with no outside window, separated from the medical room and a busy corridor by a thin partition. She insisted, as she had with the EWO the evening before, that she had nothing against either of the teachers; in fact she thought Keith Tyson was "real nice, sir, he tries to help you and that". At first she would give no explanation for her truancy, but eventually explained with obvious embarrassment that she was afraid of hurting herself in these two lessons. "It was the same last term with cookery, sir, I hardly ever went but nobody noticed then!" Coming from Kaye Milburn, this shook Donald Chester. "Hidden truancy" was something which the staff all knew existed; children came into school, got their mark on the attendance register, and left. Spot checks were held in the classes with the worst offenders, but he doubted whether anyone would have done one with Kaye's class, and even if they had it would probably not have been on Kaye's cookery day.

Kaye could not explain why she was afraid of having an accident, and in bewilderment Donald Chester asked her how many brothers and sisters she had, hoping that there might be some clue in the family. Kaye, it appeared, only had one brother, and he was nearly two years old. She was clearly fond of David, but preferred not to take him out with her to the shops "in case he ran off and had an accident, sir". A few moments later she added that she had once had a baby sister, but she had died when only six months old. Kaye sounded anxious as she said this, and feeling slightly puzzled Donald asked what had happened to this sister. Kaye replied: "I don't know, but me mum said she had an accident, and had gone to heaven."

Subsequent inquiries showed that Kaye's sister did not die in an accident; she had died of pneumonia following a severe attack of 'flu, but Mrs Milburn admitted to having told her daughter that it had been an accident: "You see, we didn't call the doctor till the morning, and I thought it would be easier for her to understand it that way," she explained. Donald Chester and the EWO suspected that Kaye had not really been fooled; nevertheless there was sufficient doubt in her mind to make her excessively frightened that she, too, might have an accident. Working on the assumption that children can cope with what they know, but not with their anxieties about things they don't know, they asked Mrs Milburn to tell Kaye what had really happened to her sister. Mrs Milburn agreed readily. "If you think that's what's right, that's what I'll do."

A few days later Kaye turned up for her woodwork lesson. After it, she said to Keith, "I know what's wrong with me now, sir; it's me little sister who died." Talking about this later in the staffroom, Keith said he reckoned there would be no more trouble with Kaye truanting. He was wrong; a few days later she again missed her PE and woodwork lessons, and was quite unable to give any explanation except that she had been afraid of hurting herself.

At this stage the school asked the advice of the visiting educational psychologist. After seeing Kaye, he said he could find no evidence that her anxiety was caused by disturbed family relationships; it probably started out as a reaction to half-felt suspicions about her sister's death; although this was no longer important, the fear of having an accident had not disappeared. The psychologist decided to "desensitise" Kaye, to help her cope with situations like woodwork, PE or cookery without feeling anxious that she might have an accident. He asked her to make a list, starting with something which made her very anxious indeed, and working down in six or seven stages to something which produced hardly any fear. He then taught her how to relax completely and asked her to imagine the least frightening thing in the list. When she could think of this without feeling any anxiety he moved on to the next one, and so to the most frightening one of all. When she was able to think of them all without having any feeling of panic, he arranged a gradual return to PE and woodwork lessons. At first the teachers were asked to be careful only to ask her to do certain very basic and straightforward tasks, but as her confidence increased they noticed that she was exceeding their instructions and joining in normally with the rest of the class.

Questions

1 Do you know other children who regularly absent themselves from a particular lesson? What are the likely reasons?

2 The EWO caused Keith Tyson and Hilda Bentley embarrassment by mentioning Kaye's absence from their lessons in the staffroom. Is the "law of the jungle" sometimes as powerful among staff as amongst children? Do

children take their lead from staff or vice versa?

3 Kaye had a habit of being overlooked; how can teachers make themselves aware of such children, especially in a secondary school where each child has eight or nine teachers in the course of the week?

4 The interview room was "a bare, boxlike place with no outside window". What does this imply about the school's priorities? How could the room be improved?

5 What arrangements can a school make to guard against "hidden truancy"? What are the alternatives to spot checks?

6 Why are adults seldom successful when they try to protect children from the truth?

7 Why might Mrs Milburn have thought it would be easier for Kaye if she said the baby had died in an accident rather than from penumonia?

8 Can you think of comparable examples when a teacher has tried to protect a child from the truth? Do you think the teacher was trying to protect the child's feelings or his own?

9 When Kaye continued to truant in woodwork and PE lessons, it might have been tempting to treat her as a malingerer; would this have been fair?

10 List some of the phobias experienced by adults you know (e.g. spiders, heights, etc.). Is there sometimes a double standard, in which adults are more tolerant towards each other's irrational fears than towards those of children?

11 Do you know any other children who might be helped in the same way as Kaye.

Derek

Main points

1 Some children are sent to special schools because they have lived down to their teacher's expectations.

2 Small schools are often less able to cater adequately for individual needs than large ones.

Everyone likes to be appreciated, and the teachers at Perry Bridge ESN infant and junior school were no exception. The Lewises were unfailingly cooperative and appreciative; they never failed to appear on the termly open day, gave their children lots of encouragement at home, sent generous contributions to the Christmas party food supply, and offered Mr Lewis's minibus when they were stuck for transport to the swimming baths or on an outing into the country. Whenever either parent accompanied the class on an expedition they were helpful and considerate to other children as well as their own. And in fact, as Mr Day, head of Perry Bridge, had reflected aloud in the staffroom, the school had done a good job with Christine and Alfie. Each of the children had been referred at the age of six in a withdrawn, inertia-like condition and a general level of language and social development more like a four-year-old; their IQs had been assessed at around 65 and this was confirmed when they were reassessed after two years. Nevertheless, both had made rapid progress in reading, and as the Lewises never tired of explaining, were doing better than Janice, who was thought to be brighter but at the age of fourteen had still not learnt to read at her local secondary school. Realising that Christine and Alfie, aged eleven and eight, could read better than her had not improved Janice's temper; she was turning into a surly, sulky adolescent, determined to protect herself from failure by not making any attempt in the first place. The Lewises were no longer worried about Christine and Alfie, but they were determined that Derek should not go the same way as Janice.

Derek was already six, and was showing no signs of academic progress. His parents had little faith in the school which had failed to teach Janice anything, but as they lived in a country district there was no alternative. They watched their youngest child's progress closely, and after a month went to the head to suggest that perhaps he ought to go to Perry Bridge with his brother and sister. Having seen Derek in his classroom (and remembering the rows over Janice who he thought should have gone to a school for maladjusted children), the head felt inclined to agree, and said he would ask for Derek to be assessed if there was still no progress by the end of the term. "Why doesn't he do it now?" grunted Miss Lamb, Derek's class teacher, when she heard. "Anyone can see he's ESN. Why waste time? It's not fair on the others."

Miss Lamb was an experienced teacher. In fact she had had thirty years of experience, twenty of them at her present school. The school's system was that the reception class teacher stayed with the children until they were ready to move into the juniors at the age of seven; teacher and children moved up the one-form entry village school together. As the head had argued to a dubious inspector, this made for stable and consistent relationships. Had he been absolutely truthful (or the inspector more perceptive), he might have admitted that the consistency was sometimes greater than the stability; and as proof of this they would have needed to look no further than the Lewis children. They had all been taught by Miss Lamb. She remembered Janice as a dull, sulky, uncooperative child, and told the remedial teacher at the comprehensive school: "I knew that child needed a special school at the age of five but nobody would do anything. Now look at her!" Christine and Alfie had been nicer children but just as dull, and she had done the right thing by having them moved into the special school; as for Derek, it was clear from the first week that he was the same. "It's genetic!" she said with a finality and assurance springing from total ignorance about inheritance.

When Miss Lamb realised that the Lewises were in complete agreement with her that Derek should go to Perry Bridge she badgered the head to ring up Mr Day and ask if he would come and have a look at him. Mr Day already knew about Derek, as Mr Lewis had visited only two days before to ask if he would arrange for his son to change schools. Welcoming the chance to establish a good relationship with a junior school in his area, Mr Day visited the following week and was suitably appalled by Derek's level of social and academic development, reflected in his apparent inability to cope with any classroom activities. He left one of his colleagues, Evelyn Statham, in the classroom while he went to talk to Derek's head teacher. Before leaving the school he promised to reserve Derek a place in Evelyn Statham's class at Perry Bridge, and said he would admit him as soon as the formalities were completed.

In the car on the way back Evelyn Statham said, "I didn't get much of a chance to say so just now, but I'm not sure that Derek is ESN. I know his teacher is determined that he is, and that his parents want him to come to us, but I don't think he's ever been given a chance at that school." Mr Day had to admit that he had been so appalled by the way Derek obviously felt, and was, ignored and lost in Miss Lamb's classroom that he had felt disinclined to ask too many questions. While the two heads had been talking, Evelyn had been working with Derek. In ten minutes she found that when she taught him how to hold his pencil he was able to copy letters accurately; he was even able to copy his name without error when she got him to tackle it letter by letter. He had drawn a man with more detail than most of the children in her class at Perry Bridge, and with only a little help he had been able to count up to ten, touching a row of building blocks as he counted. Yet Miss Lamb had shown her shapeless scribbles as evidence of his best attempts at writing and drawing, and claimed that he was quite incapable of counting except up to five by rote. Mr Day replied, "If she's that bad, he'll be better off with us whether he's ESN or not; but we'll have to wait and see what the doctor and psychologist say."

The doctor found nothing physically wrong with Derek. The psychologist confirmed everything that Evelyn Statham had said, and eventually concluded that Derek was below average in general intelligence, but certainly above the level of almost all children at Perry Bridge. He needed no one to tell him that Miss Lamb would not accept this. He had a clear choice between recommending that Derek stay with Miss Lamb for another year and a half and recommending a transfer to the ESN school. The choice was complicated by two considerations. First, he was less happy about Christine and Alfie than their teachers and parents. Although they could read, they had almost no number concept, and outside the supportive special school setting they were as immature socially and emotionally as they had ever been. This was not helped by their parents who kept them inside so that the other children could not tease them for going to "the daft school". Second, he knew that if Derek once entered Perry Bridge it might well be for a long time. The school had a protective attitude towards its pupils, and even if a child's academic attainments were demonstrably up to the level required by any primary or secondary school in the authority, there were often other good reasons against a return to normal school. Indeed Perry Bridge ESN secondary school (to which almost all pupils transferred at eleven) had started some CSE courses, because, as the head pointed out, they got on better there than in a large comprehensive!

Derek went to Perry Bridge at the start of the following term. The decision was taken after the psychologist, Mr Day and Evelyn Statham had talked for over an hour and eventually agreed to aim at teaching him the basic skills and building up his confidence in the next year and a half, with the intention of returning him to normal school when he would move out of Miss Lamb's class into the junior department. In addition, a social worker was asked to visit Mr and Mrs Lewis regularly.

Questions

1 As a class teacher what would you do about a child who was being overtaken by a younger brother?

2 Do you know other children who are "determined to protect themselves from failure by not making any attempt in the first place"? How can such children be helped?

3 What were the odds against Derek making a good start at his infant school?

4 What can a head teacher and class teacher do to prevent a child starting his school life with a handicap caused by the notoriety of his brothers and sisters?

5 Have you seen a secondary school child's progress being affected by the reputation of his older brothers and sisters?

6 Are any of Miss Lamb's attitudes reflected in your own teaching?

7 How could Derek's needs have been met more effectively if he had lived in a large town? Would the psychologist's choice have been so limited?

8 Why do you think Christine and Alfie were still so immature socially and emotionally? Would you describe their older sister, Janice, in this way?

9 Should Mr Day try to persuade Derek's parents not to keep Christine and Alfie inside, to avoid other children teasing them?

10 How can a large comprehensive school ensure that every child is known well by at least one or two teachers? Is the head of Perry Bridge ESN secondary school necessarily right to keep some of his brighter pupils because they got on better there than at a large comprehensive?

11 Do you agree with the recommendation for Derek to go to Perry Bridge?

Adrian

Main points

1 Parents, doctors and teachers are often evasive to a child about illness or physical handicap, yet the child generally senses any deception.

2 Children can cope with what they know and understand, but not with their anxieties about things they do not understand.

3 The pastoral care staff at a school should be sensitive to behavioural and emotional problems which may accompany physical handicap.

Adrian Fellows joined Bridge End Comprehensive with a good record from his junior school; he was said to be hardworking and conscientious, perhaps not very outgoing, and a little withdrawn. He had a few close friends, but he did not join in the many out-of-school activities. In his first three years at the comprehensive school he continued to make steady, though unexceptional academic progress. His teacher saw no reason to regard him as a child with special needs or difficulties, and for his part Adrian was quite happy at school. He seemed in general to be a boy of perfectly normal educational, social and emotional adjustment; he had enjoyed good health, apart from a history of *petit mal* before starting school.

When he was fourteen he developed more severe epilepsy. His mother found him unconscious in his bedroom at ten o'clock one evening, and naturally called the ambulance in a panic. Adrian had three more fits the following week, and spent a fortnight as a hospital inpatient, having a battery of tests. An electroencephelogram record of his brainwaves showed a pattern that is characteristic of epilepsy. He was accordingly placed on medication and the frequency of the fits quickly fell off, eventually stabilising at around one or two a fortnight. Adrian's teachers were informed about the epilepsy and advised what they should do if it occurred in school. However, Adrian never had fits at school; he still looked a normal, healthy attractive boy who was eager to join in games and PE.

Some three months after Adrian's discharge from hospital his class teacher was asked by a colleague whether he had noticed any change in Adrian recently. His first reaction was to say no, but thinking about it more carefully he realised that there had indeed been a slow but definite change. Adrian was becoming less cheerful and cooperative; he now sat at the back of the classroom instead of the front; he seldom went up to talk to staff; he seemed to be drifting away from his small circle of friends, without replacing them with anyone else. When his class teacher asked him if anything was wrong he gave a faint smile, and insisted politely but firmly that everything was quite all right.

A week later things were certainly not all right; Adrian was brought to the head by a young teacher who said that he had violently attacked another boy during the dinner break. When questioned Adrian readily admitted the attack, and said it was because the other boy had called him names. On further inquiry it turned out that the other boy had been one of Adrian's former friends; he claimed to be utterly bewildered by the attack, saying indignantly, "But I only called him a silly sod!" Adrian's behaviour during and after the argument worried the head far more than the fight itself; when he had been brought to his office he had still been beside himself with rage, eyes staring, body shaking, fists tightly clenched, and quite unable to listen to reason or argument. After half an hour he had calmed down enough to return to his class, but remained tense and on edge throughout the afternoon.

The head and class teacher decided to send for Adrian's parents; his mother turned up the next day, apologising, rather abrasively, that her husband could not come because he was at work. The two teachers felt that Mrs Fellows was a prickly, suspicious woman who was terribly defensive about Adrian. "I hear our Adrian's been fighting," she said. "Well, perhaps it will teach that Alfie to keep his big mouth shut; he's always opening it too loud!" The head explained tactfully that Adrian's teachers had been worried that he no longer seemed so settled and happy at school, and things had come to a head with his fight with Alfie. Mrs Fellows promptly insisted that the other boys were victimising him because of his epilepsy. "And I can tell you another thing," she told them, "he's not going to any special school for stupid kids. Our Adrian's not stupid even if he does have fits!"

The interview was not a success. Wondering where he went from here the head telephoned the school's medical officer, who wrote to the consultant who was treating Adrian at the local hospital. He wrote back saying that he could see no reason why Adrian should not be behaving normally for most of the time. It was not at all clear why the epilepsy had started in the first place, and he could not give any outlook. At best, Adrian's fits would gradually become less frequent and eventually disappear altogether; at worst they might become a good deal more frequent but in this case there were further anticonvulsant drugs which should be able to control them. He did point out though that Adrian might be feeling a good deal of self-consciousness and anxiety about his condition and asked the school to be tolerant. "It's all very well asking us to be tolerant," said the head dryly to Adrian's class teacher, "but what on earth can we do to help the kid?"

The school did not have a fulltime counsellor but one of the remedial teachers had been on several short courses in counselling and was generally acknowledged to have a "way" with difficult children. Mrs Dobb agreed to see Adrian; after explaining that this would be a confidential interview, she gave Adrian a list containing many of the common problems which trouble children and adolescents, and asked him to read through it underlining the ones which applied to him. Adrian read through the list slowly, without underlining a single item. When he got to the end he went back to the beginning again, and then slowly and deliberately underlined three items. These were: "worried about the future", "getting a good job", "girl-friend". Mrs Dobb asked which was the worst. Adrian's reply was to put his hands on his head, with an air of complete hopelessness. Mrs Dobb wondered whether Adrian was having girl-friend trouble; however, it gradually became clear that he had not had a row with his girl-friend. In fact, he had never had a steady girl-friend, and he denied wanting one now. Mrs Dobb felt understandably confused, but when she said so Adrian gave her that pitying look of anger and exasperation which adolescents reserve for uncomprehending adults. Mrs Dobb changed the subject. "Is it your own future that you are worried about?" she asked. Adrian nodded silently. In the course of the next few interviews Adrian started, slowly at first but then with greater intensity, to tell Mrs Dobb about the things which had been worrying him. Would he be able to live a normal life? How would he ever be able to get a job when he might throw a fit at any time? How would he ever be able to get a girl-friend, let alone to marry and have a family? He was disgusted by his own lack of control, so it followed that everybody else must find him disgusting too. Neither his doctor nor his parents had ever told him anything about his illness except that he must take the pills. He knew it was serious because of his mother's attitude to him; she used to be brusque and businesslike but now she always defended him. He feared that he would be the laughing-stock of the school, both teachers and children, if he made a show of himself by having a fit in school.

Slowly and painstakingly Mrs Dobb tried to reassure him. She asked Adrian to make a list of friends and former friends, and found that one of them suffered from severe eczema. Adrian said that he felt sorry for him, and that it didn't really make much difference one way or the other. "Then why should your occasional fits?" she asked. Mrs Dobb arranged for Adrian to see the school doctor, to be told in simple terms what epilepsy was and how it could be treated. He asked about the outlook and was given an honest answer; arrangements were made for him to meet two teachers from other schools who had also suffered from mild epilepsy while they were adolescent. Adrian's teachers noticed a gradual improvement but he remained moody and tense and there were two more aggressive outbursts. Then, about nine months after the first attack he had a fit in school. Fortunately the teacher concerned remembered what to do, and was able to enlist the help of two of Adrian's friends. When Adrian next saw Mrs Dobb he was looking cheerful. He explained, "You know, they're still talking to me!"

Questions

1 Adrian's teachers were informed about his epilepsy and advised what to do if he had a fit in school. Should they have known without being told? What is a school's responsibility in the event of accidents or illness? Should there be a first aid specialist on the staff?

2 Apart from learning what to do if he had a fit in school, what else might Adrian's teachers have done when they heard he had developed epilepsy?

3 What is the first aid for epilepsy?

4 After three months Adrian was sitting at the back of the class instead of the front. Are there any disadvantages in children being encouraged to sit where they want to? How can the teacher guard against them?

5 When first questioned, Adrian told his class teacher that everything was all right. Could the teacher have made any further inquiries? If a child insists that he has no worries, is it the school's business to interfere?

6 Why do you think Adrian attacked his former friend?

7 How might the head have made his interview with Adrian's mother more of a success?

8 Neither the head nor the school medical officer appear to have considered the possibility of Adrian going to a special school. Should they have? How might this have affected him?

9 The school did not have a full-time counsellor. Are there any dangers in a school having one?

10 If you had been in Mrs Dobb's place, would you have insisted on anything before agreeing to see Adrian?

11 What implications does Adrian's epilepsy have for vocational guidance?

12 What are the implications for advising him on choice of school courses?

13 Do you know of any other instances in which parents, doctors or teachers have not told a child the full facts about his illness? How much should a child be told? Who should tell him?

14 Why do you think Adrian's doctors and parents had not told him anything about his illness?

15 How can a child sense that adults are concealing something?

16 Could the school have done anything to help Adrian's mother? Should Mrs Dobb have talked to her?

17 What do you think about a policy of keeping handicapped children in a normal school? How far should a school go in order to cater for a handicapped (or difficult) child?

Joseph and Gary

Main points

1 Twins are too often thought of together instead of as individuals.

2 Parents are more likely to place exces-sive academic pressure on their children when they lack confidence in what is being done at school.

Joseph and Gary Blakeley were identical twins. Their parents could tell them apart, and so could their class teacher, remedial teacher, and a few of their friends. Most people, though, both adults and children, were hopelessly confused. To make it worse, they dressed alike; the head teacher's request that they should not wear identical clothes had not helped as there never seemed to be any consistent pattern to the differences. As well as looking and dressing alike, they behaved alike and did everything together, even when it came to having accidents and getting into trouble. A day after Gary had been knocked over by a motor-cycle and cut his eye open Joseph fell off his bicycle and broke his nose; if Joseph was taken to task for something one day, Gary was certain to be found doing the same thing the next. They had always been in the same class, and although their teachers had often thought about separating them, they had always con-sidered it unfair to penalise the children for looking alike. When they were behaving well, they were referred to as the terrible twins.

Shortly after the start of their second year at Bestwick Junior School, the twins presented their teachers with two problems (and it was perhaps not irrelevant that both Derek Lane and Mary Swann, class and remedial teachers respectively, thought they had two problems rather than four). The first was that they were making minimal progress in number, and the second was that they had been stealing at school and at home. Bestwick school prided itself on its close and harmonious contact with parents, and encouraged them to come into their children's classrooms first thing in the morning and last thing in the afternoon.

In fact it was Mrs Blakeley who had first brought up the question of the twins stealing, before their teachers had suspected anything. She had asked, rather abrasively, whether any exercise books had gone missing, and had then produced three exercise books and a collection of rubbers and pencils. "Are you going to punish them, or am I ?" she demanded. Derek Lane got out of an uncomfortable situation by suggesting that this was something which should be discussed with the head, who was at a conference and would not be returning until the following afternoon. He took advantage of the breathing space to check on the twins' records. At their last medical examination they had been declared completely fit, but in their first two years they had missed a lot of school with bronchitis and asthma. At the age of six they had been referred to a consultant physician at the local hospital, and since then their health had improved steadily. When they left the infant school their head teacher had noted: "Minimal attainments in the basic subjects due to illness; health now improving, and should be capable of good progress." In the first year and a quarter at the junior school this optimism had not been altogether justified; despite remedial help twice a week for the last two terms their arithmetic age was still less than six.

When Mrs Blakeley visited the school the next day she brought her husband with her. It quickly became clear that they wanted to talk about the twins' academic progress as well as their stealing. It was equally clear that they held the school largely responsible for both problems. "They shouldn't be doing cookery and needlework when they can't do simple sums," Mrs Blakeley said impatiently, "and why didn't anyone know these things were missing?" The head believed in encouraging his teachers to play a major part in interviews with parents (a policy which not all of them welcomed), but decided he should answer this criticism himself. Before he could do so, however, Mr Blakeley had explained that he thought it was a good thing for boys to do cookery and needlework, as a reward for good work in the important subjects like reading and maths! Further questioning revealed that Mr Blakeley spent an hour each night trying to help the twins with their number. Both he and they found this frustrating and it usually ended with them in tears and him losing his temper, shouting, and shaking them. Mary Swann asked what book he used, remembering that the twins often took their number books home. "I just give them the easy bits out of sums I make up for them," he said. "I try and get them to learn their tables but they just don't remember even the easiest ones." "Such as?" asked Mary Swann, and was not surprised by the answer: "Last night he got stuck on 'six times nine'; even though I'd told him a dozen times before, he still couldn't remember!"

Switching to the twins' stealing, the head found that at home they mostly stole food, although Mrs Blakeley had missed some money the previous week. Both parents were at work when the twins arrived home from school; their mother did not get home until an hour later, by which time they had often helped themselves to tins of fruit in the larder, even though they knew they would be having their tea as soon as their mother got in. It seemed to the teachers that Mr and Mrs Blakeley were so conscious of all their sons' failings and misdemeanours that they must be unable to see any of their good qualities. And the effect of the spankings and shakings which seemed almost a daily part of the routine in the Blakeley household was to draw the twins even closer together, as they could only rely on each other for support and approval.

Feeling slightly helpless, the head remembered he had read a book on non-directive counselling and asked, "What would you like us to do?" Taken aback, Mrs Blakeley said he was the expert and thought he should suggest something. Turning to the twins' two teachers, the head asked if they could give Joseph and Gary exercises which they could do at home for ten minutes each evening to practise what they had covered in school. He told the Blakeleys he would only allow his teachers to do this if they promised not to spend more than ten minutes each evening on these exercises; in addition, they would have to agree to Joseph and Gary being told that ten minutes was the maximum. Derek Lane and Mary Swann would meet the Blakeleys at two-month intervals specifically to review progress. Turning to the stealing, the head asked whether the twins enjoyed swimming or going to the Saturday morning film show at the local cinema. Mrs Blakeley had replied that both activities had been stopped because they couldn't be trusted. The head then suggested that they should be allowed to go to both, but that if they were suspected of taking anything on Saturday, Sunday, Monday or Tuesday, the visit to the baths on Tuesday evening should be cancelled, and that if anything was suspected on Wednesday, Thursday or Friday, the visit to the pictures should be cancelled. Mrs Blakeley insisted that this would not work, but on her husband's insistence reluctantly agreed to give it a try. "And one more thing," said the head as they were getting up to go, "they do things together too much, and I think it would be worth putting them in different classes."

None of the teachers were optimistic – indeed they were so worried by Mrs Blakeley's attitude that they thought of asking the Social Services Department for help. Nevertheless there were no further crises. After two weeks the twins complained that they had been made to work for half an hour the night before; Mrs Swann wrote, "Ten minutes only, please!" on the next set of exercises, and there had been no further complaints. At the first two-month review Mrs Blakely conceded that things might be getting a little better; she turned up for the second shortly after getting a good end of term report on the twins' progress. She brought her youngest child Ian, aged six, with her. She was, she said, very satisfied with their work, and there had been no stealing since the last meeting. "And now," she said, slapping Ian's legs in a manner that appeared jocular but nearly brought tears to his eyes, "we'll have to see about this one getting a move on!"

Questions

1 Would you place twins in the same class if there was a choice?

2 Have you come across twins who do everything together, even when it comes to having accidents and getting into trouble?

3 How can a teacher help twins to look on themselves as individuals rather than looking on themselves as one of a pair?

4 Do you think Joseph and Gary should have been punished for stealing? If so, by whom?

5 Do you know other children who got off to a bad start at school owing to illness? How does this help to create a vicious circle of increasing failure in subsequent years?

6 As a class teacher would you want to play a major part in interviews with parents? Why do you think this was not welcomed by all the teachers at Bestwick Junior School?

7 Is it ever justifiable to use one subject as a reward for doing another, as Mr Blakeley suggested?

8 Why do you think Derek Lane had not heard from the twins about the nightly struggles with arithmetic? Could the fact that they were twins have had anything to do with it?

9 Why do you think the twins stole things from school and home?

10 What do you think of the suggestion that the two boys should take work home from school each evening? Do you approve of primary school children being given homework?

11 Were there any realistic alternatives to giving the twins homework? Would Mr Blakeley have accepted a request not to make them do any work in the evenings?

12 What do you think of the head's suggestion to Mr and Mrs Blakeley about their sons' stealing? Could you use a similar approach in school?

13 What might the school have hoped to achieve if they had asked the social services department for help?

14 Is there any need for the head to pass on what he had discovered about the family to the infant school?

Sally

Main points

1 How children cope with the death of a friend or relative depends largely on how the adults around them cope with it.

2 Even though failure to make progress may start as a reaction to family difficulties, social factors within the classroom may cause them to persist long after the family problems have cleared up.

3 Teachers can never assume that important information about a child's home will be passed on to them.

"It looks as though we will have to deal with this problem ourselves," remarked the head of Tipton County Junior School. "The medical officer says she's got an IQ of 95, and they'll be pleased to keep her under review!" Mrs Lock, Sally Latham's class teacher, made a face. "I dare say the doctor's right, but I'm really not interested whether her IQ is 50 or 150, all I want to know is why nothing I do ever seems to make any difference! She just sits there and waits for me or another child to come along and show her what to do; she even lets the other children dress her after PE. If she's that bright she certainly shouldn't be far and away the worst reader in the class." Tipton County School was in a local education authority which gave a low priority to the advisory services. There was a ratio of one educational psychologist to 25,000 children (compared with the recommended ratio of one to 10,000), and it would be well over six months before Sally could be seen by one. The School Medical Service was prepared to test a child's intelligence, but was seldom able to make detailed recommendations about teaching methods.

Sally was in her first term at the junior school. Mrs Lock knew that there had been problems in her infant school; her class had had four teachers in her last year there, the last one being a young martinet straight from college, who would doubtless have become a WRAC sergeant major rather than an infant school teacher if she had received appropriate vocational guidance. Mrs Lock did not normally refer children to the part-time remedial teacher until they had been with her for a term or two; she liked to see how they developed before asking for special help. She felt that Sally was different and asked her colleague to have a look at her.

Mrs Page confirmed that she had a reading age of less than five and a half, but was unable to find any obvious reasons for this. She had no difficulty in discriminating between the different letters, there were no obvious language problems, and she could copy accurately when she was made to concentrate. Her concentration, though, was not good, and if the teacher was not sitting beside her she tended to mirror-write. Mrs Page really did not think that this was at the root of Sally's difficulties. She was too polite; she never spoke except when spoken to, either by another child or by an adult; she never took the initiative in anything; the head thought she was just lazy, but she did not actively avoid work as lazy children do. The infant school's records said that she was quiet, but making some progress by the end of her first year. In her second year there was a note that she often seemed tired, though she was continuing to make progress, but in her final year none of her teachers had time to get to know her well enough to make any useful comments.

When Mrs Lock looked at Sally's medical record she found that she had suffered from chronic tonsillitis from the age of $2\frac{1}{2}$ until $4\frac{1}{2}$, when she went into hospital to have her tonsils and adenoids removed. The tonsillitis caused slight deafness, but this had cleared up shortly before she started school and there had been no indication of it since. She had suffered from bad boils when she started school, and there were two notes saying that she was still taking extra vitamins. If anything, Mrs Lock and Mrs Page felt more confused after reading Sally's medical records than before. True, boils were a sign of being run down and this might explain the remark in her second year in the infants. Again, her deafness might have led her to rely on other people more than some children do. On the other hand, she was said to have been making progress in her first two years in the infants; she certainly was not doing so now, but she did not seem tired nor was deafness any longer a problem.

Reluctantly, Mrs Lock asked the head if he would invite Sally's parents to school to discuss their daughter's progress. She was reluctant because she herself came from an impoverished area of a large industrial city, and still found it difficult talking to the articulate, confident middle-class parents at Tipton Junior School. She would secretly have preferred to be introducing up-to-date teaching methods into the sort of school in which she had herself been educated, but when her husband was offered his present job, this was the only post the authority had been able to offer her. To her surprise, it was Mr Latham who came to school the following week. He listened carefully to everything she said, and seemed genuinely grateful for the trouble the school was taking. Sally was no longer taking any medication, and her father was satisfied that there were no longer any medical worries. Things had been difficult at home for the last twelve months; first his mother died, and then, three months later, his wife's father had died. His mother's death had been sudden, and matters were complicated by his appointment as managing director of a firm which turned out to be in a dicey position; the result was that he had been working long hours and seeing little of his family, though in the last few months this had improved. In addition, his father had been acutely depressed after his wife's death, and had lived with his son and daughter-in-law for nearly six months before being able to bring himself to return home. Even now he spent every weekend with them, and invariably spent the last hour of each visit fighting back tears. His father-in-law had been ill for a long time; he lived on his own two roads away, and Mrs Latham had had to share the nursing with a sister who also lived nearby. Following her father's death she too had become depressed, probably as a result of the prolonged strain of nursing an invalid while trying to run a home in which there were already tensions caused by the presence of her husband's father. Fortunately, she had improved a great deal in the last three or four months, and though she was still taking antidepressant pills, she was becoming more like her old self every week.

Mrs Lock was startled to hear about all this. Sally never mentioned anything about home, and her father said that at home it was difficult to get her to talk about school. She asked if she had been close to her grandparents. It turned out that she had been quite close to her maternal grandfather, enjoying running errands for him, and occasionally even playing games like Happy Families or Snakes and Ladders with him. However, she had been extremely close to her paternal grandmother, in fact her father said that she had been closer to her than to either of her parents. Her grandmother's hobby was gardening, and she spent hours helping Sally with a little plot her father had dug her at the end of the garden. She had been as devoted to Sally as Sally was to her, and her grand-daughter copied her in every possible way. She even copied her calm unruffled manner, and her respectful, somewhat over-protective, attitude towards her husband. She died of a heart attack while pulling up some weeds in Sally's garden one Friday afternoon. Sally had rushed home excitedly from school, only to find her grandfather and her mother in tears in the living room. She had stood bewildered for a minute while the two adults struggled to explain to her that her grandma had gone to heaven, and then said in a dull, factual voice, "Then I'll have to look after you now!" No one saw Sally cry until some weeks after her grandmother's funeral (which it was thought better that she should not attend). Since then though, her parents had sometimes found her crying for no apparent reason, but had never been able to discover what it was about. When her grandfather was around she made a great show of being the woman of the house, but in his absence she sometimes talked about her grandmother, and on one occasion asked her father if there were gardens in heaven. On being told that there were she said, "Good, then grandma will be able to do her gardening there!"

Mr and Mrs Latham had both been worried about Sally, but felt now that she was "getting over it". They were regular churchgoers, and the vicar had advised them to encourage Sally to think about the happy things she had done with her grandmother. He had also suggested that it was not a good thing for Sally to act the part of "woman of the house" when her grandfather was present. The vicar had said that Sally must be a very strongminded little girl to control her feelings in this way; it was as though she was too frightened to show her own grief when the grown-ups so obviously could not cope with theirs. Small children often have fantasies in which they see themselves as strong and powerful, and surrounded by so much distress and depression in her relatives, and with her father frequently away at work, Sally might have been clinging desperately to her fantasy of herself as the one strong member of the family. "Things are getting a lot better now though," said Mr Latham. "Sally is starting to be noisy again, and is even starting to be naughty, but in a nice way."

Mrs Lock was sure that this interview shed a lot of light on Sally's problems at school, but was not quite sure how. Both bereavements had occurred at a particularly unsettled time for the class in her infant school, and as a result nobody had heard about them. For the same reasons Sally's teachers could not be aware of the change in her behaviour, and nor could the junior school be alerted. Under the circumstances Mrs Lock and Mrs Page decided that Sally should have some extra attention in the form of remedial help, but that no other action would be necessary as her father had reported that she was starting to improve. Unfortunately Sally's apathetic, withdrawn behaviour in school did not change over the next six months, and nor did she make any significant progress in reading or number work. At open evening in the summer term her parents cheerfully reported that she was completely back to normal, a lively, noisy girl who always wanted to play out and had plenty of friends, and was quite capable of taking the lead among her friends. This was confirmed by a parent who lived close to the Lathams, and the next day another child in class said, "She's not like this at home, you know, Miss," when she had told Sally to get out her reading book for the fourth time.

By this stage there were only three weeks of the summer term left, and Sally would be with another teacher next September. Mrs Lock felt profoundly depressed by her lack of progress with her, and had a long talk with the teacher who would be taking her class next term. Mrs Lock felt that Sally should be referred to a psychologist, but her colleague wanted to see her for himself for a few weeks before taking this step. He thought that Sally might be behaving in this way because the rest of the class expected her to. He had noticed once or twice that it was often another child who pointed out that Sally had not done something and wondered whether Sally was simply taking the easy way out by reacting to their expectations. He hoped he might bring Sally out of her shell by getting the other children to take no notice of her except when she took the initiative in something.

Questions

1 Is there anyone the head of Tipton County Junior School could have approached for advice, even though the authority had such limited advisory services?

2 What help should be available to teachers in their first year? What help or advice should have been available to Sally's last teacher in her infant school?

3 Mrs Lock liked to see how children developed before asking for special help; is this attitude likely to be shared by her next teacher? Is it sometimes a cause of indefinite procrastination in obtaining special help for a child?

4 Sally had a tendency to mirror-write when she was not concentrating; is this a cause for concern in a seven-year-old?

5 Do you agree with the head that Sally was just lazy? Do lazy children actively avoid work?

6 Mrs Lock found it hard to talk to the articulate, middle-class parents at Tipton County School. Do you find it difficult talking to parents (or children) from a different social class to yourself?

7 How do you think Sally's medical history might have contributed to her current problems?

8 If you had heard about Sally's reaction to her grandfather's death at the time, would you have seen it as a cause for concern? What would you have suggested?

9 Would you have encouraged Sally to attend her grandmother's funeral?

10 It is natural for a seven-year-old to pretend to be an adult. Why was it a reason for concern in Sally's case?

11 Do you agree with the vicar's explanation and advice to Mr and Mrs Lock?

12 What sort of remedial help did Sally need at school? Is her reading the basic problem?

13 What methods would you use to teach Sally to read, assuming you had four one-hour lessons a week with a group of five children?

14 How might it be possible to use Sally's remedial reading sessions to draw her out of her shell and increase her self-confidence?

15 How could you try to ensure that any social progress she made in the remedial group was maintained elsewhere?

16 Do you agree with the argument of Sally's next teacher? How would you set about bringing a child out of her shell "by getting the other children to take no notice of her except when she took the initiative in something"?

17 How would you explain this approach in terms of reinforcement principles?

Further Reading

Blackham, G. J. and Silberman, A., *Modification of Child Behaviour*, Wadsworth, 1971.

Bruner, J. S., *Beyond the Information Given: Studies in the Psychology of Knowing*, George Allen and Unwin, 1974.

Craft, M., Raynor, J. and Cohen, L. (eds.), *Linking Home and School*, Longman, 1972.

Daniels, J. C. and Diack, H., *The Standard Reading Tests*, Chatto and Windus, 1972.

Douglas, J. W. B., *The Home and the School*, Macgibbon and Kee, 1964.

Douglas, J. W. B., Ross, J. M. and Simpson, M. R., *All Our Future*, Peter Davies, 1968.

Eron, L. D., Walder, L. O., and Lefkowitz, M. M., *Learning of Aggression in Children*, Little, Brown and Co, 1971.

Hargreaves, D. H., Hester, S. K. and Mellor, F. J., *Deviance in the Classroom*, Routledge and Kegan Paul, 1976.

Herbert, M., *Emotional Problems of Development in Children*, Academic Press, 1974.

Holt, J., *How Children Fail*, Penguin, 1973.

Holt, J., *How Children Learn*, Penguin, 1973.

Kellmer Pringle, M., *The Needs of Children*, Hutchinson, 1974.

Kemble, B. (ed.), *Fit to Teach: A Private Inquiry into the Training of Teachers, with Recommendations*, Hutchinson, 1971.

Nash, R., *Classrooms Observed*, Routledge and Kegan Paul, 1973.

Patterson, G. R. and Gullion, M. E., *Living with Children: New Methods for Parents and Teachers*, Research Press, 1974.

Reimer, E., *School is Dead*, Penguin, 1971.

Rosenthal, R. and Jacobsen, L., *Pygmalion in the Classroom*, Holt, Rinehart and Winston, 1968.

Silberman, M. L., Allender, J. S. and Yanoff, J. M., *The Psychology of Open Teaching and Learning: An Inquiry Approach*, Little, Brown and Co, 1972.

Turner, B. (ed.), *Truancy*, Ward Lock, 1974.

Tyerman, M., *Truancy*, University of London Press, 1968.

Index